# OURSELVES & THE COMMUNITY

# OURSELVES AND THE COMMUNITY

BY

E. E. REYNOLDS

THIRD AND REVISED EDITION

CAMBRIDGE
AT THE UNIVERSITY PRESS
1950

CAMBRIDGE UNIVERSITY PRESS
Cambridge, New York, Melbourne, Madrid, Cape Town,
Singapore, São Paulo, Delhi, Tokyo, Mexico City

Cambridge University Press
The Edinburgh Building, Cambridge CB2 8RU, UK

Published in the United States of America by Cambridge University Press, New York

www.cambridge.org
Information on this title: www.cambridge.org/9781107617902



First published 1950
First Edition 1932
Second Edition 1935
Reprinted 1938
Third Edition 1950
First paperback edition 2011

*A catalogue record for this publication is available from the British Library*

ISBN 978-1-107-61790-2 Paperback

# CONTENTS

CONTENTS

## THE NATIONAL COMMUNITY

## THE BRITISH COMMUNITY



## THE WORLD COMMUNITY

# PREFACE

## TO THE THIRD EDITION

There have been so many developments and changes in public affairs since 1932 when this book was first published that it has become necessary to carry out a complete revision; this has, indeed, meant rewriting the greater part.

The purpose is to supply a conspectus of political organisation, local, central and international. The book is particularly intended for the guidance of those who are looking forward to the time when their names will be on the register of electors. It is however hoped that it will prove useful to all who approach these subjects for the first time and need a sketch-map of the field of inquiry.

Although many subjects come within the scope of the book, others of vital concern to all citizens have been omitted. Nothing, for instance, has been said about the economic life of the country, nor about banking, nor of the social structure. It seemed impossible to say anything useful about these and other topics in a brief outline, and any attempt to do so would have complicated an already rather congested scheme of study. The book, therefore, is limited to a consideration of the machinery of government; emphasis has been put on the historical development of the parts of the constitution; experience shows that this is not only interesting in itself but is an aid to understanding the nature of the present organisation.

The four chapters headed "How we can help" include suggestions for further reading with some subjects for consideration and discussion.

The books mentioned are, in the main, volumes best suited for following up the topics sketched in these pages. Most of these books contain suggestions for more advanced study. For the most part those recommended are inexpensive and are likely to be in print. A few more expensive volumes of outstanding importance are such as can be found in any decent public library.

The suggestions for discussion and inquiry are designed to assist the individual reader and also study groups or teams. Even a team of two can do more profitable work in these subjects than a solitary student by himself; exchange of opinion, argument on principles, and the discussion of difficult points all help to ensure a clearer understanding.

A larger group, say of five or six, can make a more thorough study by dividing inquiries amongst themselves and then pooling the results. It is important to avoid having too many members of a group; they should be able to sit round an ordinary table, each taking it in turns to be the host and chairman. Too much formality is to be avoided but the usual rules of debate should be observed to avoid waste of time in pointless talk. A few subjects for elementary research are suggested, but others will soon occur to the members of any live group. Nor should the value of visits be overlooked—the local Council, a sitting of Petty Sessions, a newspaper office, and so on. If a few days can be spent in London there might be visits to the Law Courts, the Houses of Parliament, the Imperial Institute, etc.

It will also be found useful to invite men of experience to meet the group, such as a local Councillor, a Trade Union official, the Medical Officer, or the Education Secretary. Such people are generally glad to meet intelligent inquirers and explain their work and answer questions.

E. E. R.

*January* 1950

*The diagram on p. 197 is reproduced by permission of His Majesty's Stationery Office*

# OURSELVES & THE COMMUNITY

## CHAPTER I

## CITIZENSHIP

### i. *The Good Citizen*

Citizen is one of those words we use rather loosely without perhaps thinking out its full meaning. We all know vaguely what it means; it implies membership of an organised community; perhaps it would be more correct to say membership of several communities, for as no man can live entirely by himself, neither can he restrict his relationships to the immediate village or town in which he happens to live.

When Paul declared, "I am a Jew, of Tarsus in Cilicia, a citizen of no mean city", he was taking a natural pride in his membership of two communities, his nation and his native town. It will be remembered that when he was brought before Festus he said, "I appeal unto Caesar". He was then acknowledging even a third citizenship, that of Rome, the capital of the Empire. So one of us might say, "I am a citizen of London, of Great Britain, and of the British Commonwealth of Nations". From this it is clear that the meaning of the word cannot be confined to our immediate community, but passes beyond to larger societies that have claims upon our loyalty and attachment.

After Nansen's death he was referred to as "a nationalist to the core; he was also a European, a citizen of the world society". Here is a still wider meaning the word has acquired during recent times. "Citizen of the world" would have meant nothing to Saxon or Dane; it is now used to denote a man whose horizon is not limited by his town, or even by his country, but stretches out to the ends of the world.

We must therefore be careful to avoid a parish-pump kind of citizenship. This does not mean ignoring the parish pump altogether; that way lies anarchy, for if we are incapable of looking after our own immediate community we shall certainly not be in a position to play a useful part in a wider field. Our citizenship begins indeed in our own homes.

Our first business is to see that we support ourselves, and our families, so that we do not become a liability to the nation instead of an asset. We should set before ourselves the ideal of independence, not in the sense of freedom from work, but from outside assistance in keeping ourselves and those dependent upon us. The independent man, however poor his circumstances may be, treasures his self-respect and the accompanying peace and strength of mind and spirit. The individual's self-respect and self-reliance are the basic elements of a sound civic life, just as they form the foundation of a sound character.

The kind of community to be found in any country depends largely on what most of its members regard as the best qualities of character and the most estimable forms of conduct. It is for this reason that each of us has an important share in society. At times it is tempting to say, "What do I matter—just one individual amongst forty millions?" This is a narrow view. Suppose, for instance, you were to decide that keeping *your* word is not of very much importance; what does it matter, you may argue, if just one person out of so great a multitude breaks a promise or a contract? You are really assuming that all the others will not break their promises; but if you do, why shouldn't they? If they followed your example, no one would be able to trust anyone else—the result would be a breakdown of social and commercial relations. Or, consider the important business of electing our representatives to local Councils and to Parliament. If too many of us say, "My vote is of no importance", then we may get Councillors and M.P.s of a kind that would do more harm than good, and we shall certainly have no right to grumble at the result of our want of a sense of responsibility.

Thus the character of each of us is important; a community of self-supporting, responsible citizens, with high standards of dealings between themselves and a desire to help one another, is an ideal to which each of us can contribute something.

It is also important that we should keep physically healthy. This is not something the community does for us completely; good sanitary conditions are, of course, an aid, but each must do his own part in looking after his own general health. A National Health Service does not replace personal responsibility.

In *Erewhon* Samuel Butler describes an imaginary country where to be ill is a crime, for illness means inefficiency. Something of this attitude would not come amiss in this country; there are people who "enjoy bad health"; fortunately most of us are too busy to share their morbid pleasures. Our trouble is rather different; we are so busily occupied in earning our bread and butter that we overlook the need for keeping the machinery in order. This necessitates maintaining an even balance of work and play; overworking where it is avoidable can be as unsocial as over-indulgence in recreation. Our play may take the form of outdoor activities suited to our age, or it may take the form of change of occupation, but the balance must be kept, otherwise a breakdown is inevitable, and we then become a burden, instead of a support, to the community.

We must keep ourselves not only physically but mentally fit. Modern life is full of difficult problems; the useful citizen is the man who can keep his head clear and develop the habit of thinking out the questions of the hour without being rushed by the latest newspaper stunt or by self-advertising quacks. Now clear thinking is a matter of self-training just as much as physical fitness. The man who is going to take part in a race does not wait until the eleventh hour before he begins his training; nor should anyone wait until the eve of the poll before making up his mind how to vote; it is too late then, he will be unbalanced by the emotionalism of the hour. Much careful study and hard thinking are needed, but unless we are prepared to give these we have no right to grumble when things go wrong. We must prepare ourselves for our task. It is no use saying that we are not interested in these affairs: the mere fact that we live in a community and share its benefits necessarily means that we are involved willy nilly in its government; we have no choice in the matter, for even if we refuse to exercise the vote, we may by so doing produce an even greater effect than if we went to the polling booth. The good citizen accepts these responsibilities, and recognises the duty of taking up his share of the work.

It is important to stress the fact that "taking up his share of the work" does not mean necessarily taking an active part in local or central government. Not all have the aptitude or the time for such labour; we shall be doing our part if we become informed citizens; not content with delegating the thinking as well as the management of the community to others and so trying to shuffle off our responsibility. It is of equal importance that every elector should understand local and public affairs, so that he can take an intelligent interest in the life of the community, and exercise his franchise with discrimination and thoughtfulness. Those who have the gifts necessary for public work should have our gratitude and our sympathy; too often they are the objects of our discontent, which should more frequently be directed at ourselves for not giving the best of our thoughts to public affairs.

The first stage is getting to know how our various communities are governed; how they affect the individual and how they react one on another. The pages that follow attempt to give an outline of such information. But it must be remembered that this is merely the skeleton of the body politic; just as the medical student has to learn anatomy before he can diagnose and heal, so the citizen must know the anatomy of society before he can hope to influence it for good. No attempt should be made to 'learn up' the subject at a few sittings. A hurried reading will merely lead to confusion of thought and a feeling of despair. Study each chapter separately and think out some of the questions suggested before breaking fresh ground. In this way knowledge will be built up gradually, and each section consolidated before the next is begun.

## ii. *Duties and Rights*

The word 'community' has been frequently used in the previous pages; if we speak too often of the 'State' or of the 'Government'[1] we are apt to think of these as things apart from ourselves. In our kind of society we are all responsible members of the State; it was Louis XIV who said, "L'État, c'est moi", and he was stating a fact since he had sufficient personal power to shape and control the government of France. Such absolute monarchy is so rare to-day that we have to think for a time before we can give an example. A new kind of absolute control has come into existence during this century; it is the absolutism of a party or group that refuses, once it has gained power, to allow any opposition or even adverse criticism. To this kind of government the ugly name 'totalitarianism' has been given; the first part 'total' indicates the meaning of the whole word.

The type of government to which we belong in Great Britain has the general term 'democratic' applied to it. Many other European countries, such as France, Holland, Belgium,

[1] In this book when 'Government' is spelled with an initial capital it means the Ministry in office; a small initial 'g' has the wider meaning of the whole body of authority.

and the Scandinavian countries are also democratic. No two of these have exactly the same form of government; France, for instance, has no king, while several of the others have kings. So the word 'democratic' does not describe any one constitution. A democratic community can be recognised by certain characteristics which may be found present in a republic like the United States of America, or in a monarchy like Norway. Perhaps the most important mark is freedom of discussion; we can argue or grumble in our homes, or in the train, or indeed anywhere, provided we do not create a disturbance; our newspapers can criticise the Government of the day and public meetings can be held to discuss or promote any subject; the police may be present or at hand, but only to step in if arguments give way to violence. A second distinguishing mark of a democracy is that periodically the citizens elect representatives to the local Councils and to Parliament; voting is carried out in secret so that no man's vote is known unless he himself reveals how he voted. Candidates can be put forward by any parties, or they can stand as independents. A third mark, and a most important one, is that in a democracy the law is applied with strict impartiality; the judges are quite independent of the Government of the day; nor can any citizen be imprisoned without being quickly brought to trial in open court.

These, and other, characteristics are based on the fact that each individual has certain RIGHTS as a citizen. In this country there is no one document or law setting out our Rights; they have been established for us by our forefathers after long struggles but without such a violent revolution as that in France in 1789 or in Russia in 1917. There are certain milestones, as we may call them, along the road of democracy we have followed; such are Magna Carta of 1215, the Great Parliament of 1295, the Petition of Right of 1628, the Bill of Rights of 1689, the Act of Settlement of 1701, and the Reform Act of 1832.

## HUMAN RIGHTS

The French National Assembly in 1789 made a Declaration of Rights that has become famous; it now seems a rather commonplace document, but at the time it terrified the other Governments of Europe. On 10 December 1948, the General Assembly of the United Nations (see p. 211) proclaimed a Universal Declaration of Human Rights. This was supported by forty-eight of the member States; none opposed it, but nine did not vote. It must be remembered that this Declaration is not a law that can be enforced in all countries; it is really a statement of an ideal towards which the countries concerned agree to work; no one of them can claim that all these rights are yet established. Although this document is rather long, it is so important that it must be given in full.

*Article 1*

All human beings are born free and equal in dignity and rights. They are endowed with reason and conscience and should act towards one another in a spirit of brotherhood.

*Article 2*

(1) Everyone is entitled to all the rights and freedoms set forth in this Declaration, without distinction of any kind, such as race, colour, sex, language, religion, political or other opinion, national or social origin, property, birth or other status.

(2) Furthermore, no distinction shall be made on the basis of the political, jurisdictional or international status of the country or territory to which a person belongs, whether this territory be an independent, Trust, Non-Self-Governing territory, or under any other limitation of sovereignty.

*Article 3*

Everyone has the right to life, liberty and the security of person.

*Article 4*

No one shall be held in slavery or servitude; slavery and the slave trade shall be prohibited in all their forms.

*Article 5*

No one shall be subjected to torture or to cruel inhuman or degrading treatment or punishment.

## CITIZENSHIP

*Article* 6

Everyone has the right to recognition everywhere as a person before the law.

*Article* 7

All are equal before the law and are entitled without any discrimination to equal protection of the law. All are entitled to equal protection against any discrimination in violation of this Declaration and against any incitement to such discrimination.

*Article* 8

Everyone has the right to an effective remedy by the competent national tribunals for acts violating the fundamental rights granted him by the constitution or by law.

*Article* 9

No one shall be subjected to arbitrary arrest, detention or exile.

*Article* 10

Everyone is entitled in full equality to a fair and public hearing by an independent and impartial tribunal, in the determination of his rights and obligations and of any criminal charge against him.

*Article* 11

(1) Everyone charged with a penal offence has the right to be presumed innocent until proved guilty according to law in a public trial at which he has had all the guarantees necessary for his defence.

(2) No one shall be held guilty of any penal offence on account of any act or omission which did not constitute a penal offence, under national or international law, at the time when it was committed. Nor shall a heavier penalty be imposed than the one that was applicable at the time the penal offence was committed.

*Article* 12

No one shall be subjected to arbitrary interference with his privacy, family, home or correspondence, nor to attacks upon his honour and reputation. Everyone has the right to the protection of the law against such interference or attacks.

*Article* 13

(1) Everyone has the right to freedom of movement and residence within the borders of each state.

(2) Everyone has the right to leave any country, including his own, and to return to his country.

*Article* 14

(1) Everyone has the right to seek and to enjoy in other countries asylum from persecution.

(2) This right may not be invoked in the case of prosecutions genuinely arising from non-political crimes or from acts contrary to the purposes and principles of the United Nations.

*Article* 15

(1) Everyone has the right to a nationality.

(2) No one shall be arbitrarily deprived of his nationality nor denied the right to change his nationality.

*Article* 16

(1) Men and women of full age, without any limitation due to race, nationality or religion, have the right to marry and to found a family. They are entitled to equal rights as to marriage, during marriage and at its dissolution.

(2) Marriage shall be entered into only with the free and full consent of the intending spouses.

(3) The family is the natural and fundamental group unit of society and is entitled to protection by society and the State.

*Article* 17

(1) Everyone has the right to own property alone as well as in association with others.

(2) No one shall be arbitrarily deprived of his property.

*Article* 18

Everyone has the right to freedom of thought, conscience and religion; this right includes freedom to change his religion or belief, and freedom, either alone or in community with others and in public or private, to manifest his religion or belief in teaching, practice, worship and observance.

*Article* 19

Everyone has the right to freedom of opinion and expression; this right includes freedom to hold opinions without interference and to seek, receive and impart information and ideas through any media and regardless of frontiers.

*Article* 20

(1) Everyone has the right to freedom of peaceful assembly and association.

(2) No one may be compelled to belong to an association.

## CITIZENSHIP

*Article* 21

(1) Everyone has the right to take part in the government of his country, directly or through freely chosen representatives.

(2) Everyone has the right of equal access to public service in his country.

(3) The will of the people shall be the basis of the authority of government; this will shall be expressed in periodic and genuine elections which shall be by universal and equal suffrage and shall be held by secret vote or by equivalent free voting procedures.

*Article* 22

Everyone, as a member of society, has the right to social security and is entitled to realisation, through national effort and international co-operation and in accordance with the organisation and resources of each State, of the economic, social and cultural rights indispensable for his dignity and the free development of his personality.

*Article* 23

(1) Everyone has the right to work, to free choice of employment, to just and favourable conditions of work and to protection against unemployment.

(2) Everyone, without any discrimination, has the right to equal pay for equal work.

(3) Everyone who works has the right to just and favourable remuneration ensuring for himself and his family an existence worthy of human dignity, and supplemented, if necessary, by other means of social protection.

(4) Everyone has the right to form and to join trade unions for the protection of his interests.

*Article* 24

Everyone has the right to rest and leisure, including reasonable limitation of working hours and periodic holidays with pay.

*Article* 25

(1) Everyone has the right to a standard of living adequate for the health and well-being of himself and of his family, including food, clothing, housing and medical care and necessary social services, and the right to security in the event of unemployment, sickness, disability, widowhood, old age or other lack of livelihood in circumstances beyond his control.

(2) Motherhood and childhood are entitled to special care and assistance. All children, whether born in or out of wedlock, shall enjoy the same social protection.

*Article* 26

(1) Everyone has the right to education. Education shall be free, at least in the elementary and fundamental stages. Elementary education shall be compulsory. Technical and professional education shall be made generally available and higher education shall be equally accessible to all on the basis of merit.

(2) Education shall be directed to the full development of the human personality and to the strengthening of respect for human rights and fundamental freedoms. It shall promote understanding, tolerance and friendship among all nations, racial or religious groups, and shall further the activities of the United Nations for the maintenance of peace.

(3) Parents have a prior right to choose the kind of education that shall be given to their children.

*Article* 27

(1) Everyone has the right freely to participate in the cultural life of the community, to enjoy the arts and to share in scientific advancement and its benefits.

(2) Everyone has the right to the protection of the moral and material interests resulting from any scientific, literary or artistic production of which he is the author.

*Article* 28

Everyone is entitled to a social and international order in which the rights and freedoms set forth in this Declaration can be fully realised.

*Article* 29

(1) Everyone has duties to the community in which alone the free and full development of his personality is possible.

(2) In the exercise of his rights and freedoms, everyone shall be subject only to such limitations as are determined by law solely for the purpose of securing due recognition and respect for the rights and freedoms of others and of meeting the just requirements of morality, public order and the general welfare in a democratic society.

(3) These rights and freedoms may in no case be exercised contrary to the purposes and principles of the United Nations.

*Article* 30

Nothing in this Declaration may be interpreted as implying for any State, group or person any right to engage in any activity or to perform any act aimed at the destruction of any of the rights and freedoms set forth herein.

Each of the above Articles might be the subject of a debate; in this way we should get a better understanding of the Declaration and of its implications.

The fact that we are all members of the community implies not only that we have RIGHTS, but that we have DUTIES. We may briefly summarise the most important here. First is the duty of living an upright life. This has already been touched upon, but it cannot be too often stressed that the value of a country is measured by the standard of morality and of character of its individual citizens.

We must observe law and order. No doubt occasions may arise when there is a conflict of loyalties; personal conscience must then be our guide; but in this country we have many ways of expressing grievances and constitutional methods of redressing them; these must be followed, and past history shows that they generally are successful in the long run, however tedious the waiting may prove to the enthusiast.

We must be ready to bear our share of the expense of organising the State. There are many services provided that touch our health and comfort; we must recognise that these have to be paid for and that it is our duty to do our part in meeting the bill.

We must be ready, if called upon, to serve personally on Local Councils and other public bodies, and to serve on juries and other bodies for the common good. Other duties are the educating of our children, casting our votes in the elections, respecting public property, and so on.

Our RIGHTS have come to us as the result of the labours of good men in the past, not without strife and hard work. It is part of our duty to see that we pass on these unimpaired to our successors and thus set ourselves a high standard in the carrying out of our DUTIES to the State.

# THE LOCAL COMMUNITY

## CHAPTER II

## VOLUNTARY ASSOCIATIONS

Before we consider the organisation of the community for the purposes of administration, something must be said of the many voluntary associations we make amongst ourselves. These are important to us in our social life, and we are probably more aware of the local cricket club or of the amateur dramatic society than we are of the town Council. It is also to be noted that many national schemes have grown out of voluntary associations; our schools, for instance, were at one time provided by private individuals or groups of public-spirited persons; so too, the present wide scheme of National Insurance can be traced back to the Lodge of the Friendly Society meeting in the local inn. You can see both types of organisation at work in a school. By law, children have to attend school, but inside the school community there are clubs and societies of many kinds of which membership is a matter of free choice.

In the adult world there are innumerable organisations bringing neighbours together for religious, cultural or recreational purposes. The members generally manage their own affairs through elected officials and committees. Experience of this kind has provided a valuable training in government; the members have learned that if all are to enjoy the association, no one can have his own way all the time; each must be ready to listen to the views of the other members and to accept the decision of the majority—or leave the association.

## i. *Trade Unions*

In addition to these neighbourly affairs there are wider organisations, but still voluntary, concerned with the way in which we earn our livings. It is natural that such men as doctors or architects should form associations to establish codes of professional conduct and to safeguard the standards of membership. Such men, unless employed in the government or municipal service, are not dependent on an employer who pays them a fixed salary. We may call them the fee-earning group. But the majority of people are wage-earners, or salary-earners, and are employed on agreed terms. This distinction is not as clear-cut as it used to be; before this century the employer was usually a person known to his workmen, and he conducted his business himself. To-day, the employer is more usually a 'Firm' consisting of a number of shareholders who are unknown to the workmen. The business is conducted by directors and managers. This does not however affect the worker's interest in how much he is paid, nor in how many hours he works.

The problem of the conditions of labour grew acute as a result of the period of change usually known as the Industrial Revolution which may be dated from about 1760. Put very briefly this change was the passing away of agricultural England and the beginning of the period of steam power with the development of the great industries, such as coal, iron and cotton, that made this country wealthy during the nineteenth century. Unfortunately the change was so sudden that there was no time to adjust ideas on labour nor to provide decent housing to meet the new conditions. Consequently there was appalling suffering in factories and mines. Small children were herded together with men and women under conditions of work that were little short of slavery, and it was only gradually that the country awoke to the fact of the misery caused through this sudden industrial development. Much good was accomplished by Factory Acts and other legislation, but the work-people themselves felt the need for protecting their own interests against the terrible conditions under which they had to work. There were in existence many clubs of artisans, such as millwrights and masons, but this period of industrialisation led to the further development of organisations of work-people in defence of themselves.

It was unfortunate that the Napoleonic Wars following the French Revolution coincided with this industrial development. The Government became suspicious of any gatherings of work-people, and treated them as conspiracies against the State. Severe laws were passed against all 'combinations', as they were called, and attempts to bargain for better wages were made illegal. In spite of this men met together in their desperation under the cloak of social and friendly clubs; even so they did not escape persecution. As late as 1834 some agricultural labourers at Tolpuddle in Dorsetshire were sentenced to seven years transportation to Australia for trying to organise themselves in the hope of getting better wages—at that period they earned about ten shillings a week when employed full time.

Many years of bitter struggle had to be endured before the right to form Unions was granted. The strike was the only weapon the workers could use, and often the employers replied with the lock-out. The story of that struggle is too long to be told here, and one example of what could happen must suffice to remind ourselves of what had to be endured.

On 12 August 1889 the dockers of London came out on strike to get their wages raised from fivepence to sixpence an hour—the 'Dockers' Tanner'. Long processions of hungry and ragged men marched through London to make their needs known. The employers tried to bring in men from other ports, and an ugly situation was created. Public opinion was on the side of the dockers and subscriptions poured in for their support. It was not until Cardinal Manning and Lord Buxton intervened that at last the employers consented to negotiate. On 16 September agreement was reached. This strike once again showed the need for some kind of system for consultation between employers and workmen so that grievances could be discussed before a strike was called.

The first step was the Conciliation Act of 1896 which gave power to the Government to intervene in any dispute *if both parties agreed*. This was followed in 1919 by the Industrial Courts Act by which an Industrial Court was established by the Board of Trade (this matter now comes under the Ministry of Labour); the court consists of representatives of both employers and workmen under a neutral chairman. The Ministry can also appoint a Court of Inquiry to find out the facts in any dispute. By these voluntary means a large number of grievances have been remedied. If both sides want to avoid open conflict, all the necessary machinery exists for discussion and settlement. This does not mean that strikes are always avoided. Sometimes they occur against the advice of the Union officials; sometimes they happen because the men feel that negotiations have been drawn out too long. The immediate cause of a strike may seem to the onlooker to be trivial, just as the immediate occasion of a war may be a comparatively unimportant incident. Before passing judgement we should make every effort to understand the real grievance behind a strike.

By this method of consultation many matters besides wages have been discussed and improvements effected; such subjects as general working conditions, the safety of the workman, his holidays and hours of work, have all been discussed round the table to the benefit of all.

Owing to the unplanned way in which the Unions were formed, there were at one time a much larger number than at present. Several Unions might be formed in one trade or industry, each providing for a section of the workers concerned. The tendency has been for such allied Unions to join together and so gain greater bargaining power. Thus in 1896 there were 1358 Unions with a total membership of 1,608,339; fifty years later, in 1946, there were 753 Unions with a total membership of 8,714,000.

One of the factors tending towards amalgamation has been the Trade Unions Congress which has met annually since 1868. The Congress is not a governing body, for each Union manages its own affairs, but it provides a means for discussing common problems and for forming general policy. In 1900 the Congress established a Labour Representation Committee to secure the election to Parliament of those acquainted with labour problems and ideals. The first Secretary of this Committee was J. Ramsay MacDonald, who became the first Labour Prime Minister in 1924. Each Union has a political fund to which members contribute unless they claim exemption.

The influence of the Trade Unions is considerable; they are consulted by the Government in matters affecting the workers, and the increasing co-operation between employers and the Unions in matters of common interest is an important factor in the industrial life of the country.

When one thinks back to the position a hundred years ago, the progress made is astonishing. The Unions have won for their members, and for others outside the organisation, a sense of responsibility and self-respect, and the gain to the community has been enormous. As new factors come into play, such as the nationalisation of certain industries or services, so the Unions will have to consider their policies afresh and be ready to meet new situations and needs. Their past history suggests that such developments will provide them with an important role in the future of the community.

## ii. '*The Co-op*'

We must glance at another way in which the workers have by voluntary association helped to improve their conditions. The Co-operative Movement aims at providing goods at the lowest possible price to its members; any profits go back into the Society or are paid as dividends to the members. There is not one Society for the whole country; each town, or group of towns, has its own 'Co-op'.

In this country the movement dates back more than a hundred years, and in its first form is associated with the name of Robert Owen (1771–1858). His idea was that communities of workers should own land and the necessary capital for developing it and then share alike in the results of their labours. In this form co-operation had a brief success. The forerunner of the present Co-operative Societies was the band of twenty-eight Rochdale Pioneers who in 1844 scraped up a capital of one pound each and opened a store for selling provisions; interest on shares was limited to 5 per cent and all profits were divided amongst the purchasers in proportion to the amount spent on buying goods. Membership by 1857 had increased to 1850, and the capital had risen from £28 to £15,000. This became the model for similar societies that sprang up all over the country. The principle of limiting interest on shares is still maintained. Part of the surplus after the 'divi' has been paid is now used for educational and social purposes.

In 1947 there were in the United Kingdom and Northern Ireland

10,300 Co-operative retail shops under
1,118 Co-operative Societies.

The first figure may be compared with the 15,300 shops controlled by multiple stores (such as Liptons), and the 120,400 shops run by independent retailers. The total number of 'Co-op' members for 1947 was 9,805,300, and the sales totalled £434,200,000.

Since the Co-operative Societies are not run for private profit but for the mutual benefit of the members, they are registered under the Industrial and Provident Society Acts, and are consequently exempt from some forms of taxation.

The retail Co-operative Societies in England have joined to establish the Co-operative Wholesale Society. There is another for Scotland, and a third joint Society for both countries.

These wholesale societies are great manufacturing organisations, landowners and farmers. They produce such things as biscuits, jam, soap, furniture, etc.; they grow their own wheat in Canada, and have large tea plantations in the East, and palm forests in Africa.

CHAPTER III

# LOCAL GOVERNMENT AUTHORITIES

If we could be transported back in time to the Middle Ages we should find that life was not quite as merry as we sometimes think. Our noses for instance would be offended at the stench in the towns, which were without any kind of sanitation. Garbage and filth were simply thrown out into the street or anywhere else convenient, and allowed to accumulate until even the people of those days became aware of the odour and decided to shift the accumulation a bit further on. The recurrent plagues which swept over the country were the direct result of lack of sanitation and of unhealthy conditions of living. There were no lighting arrangements for the towns or villages, and when it grew dusk men closed their heavy doors, bolted and barred them, and dared not venture out for fear of robbers and cut-throats. There was no organised police, and in parts of the country thieves and robbers could pursue their evil practices for long periods undeterred by any fear of capture or punishment. Outside the towns the roads were appalling—indeed it is hardly just to call them roads in our modern sense, for they were little more than rough cart tracks, which in winter and in wet weather were often impassable, and were dangerous owing to deep pits.

This picture may seem very gloomy, and it is of course not intended to be a complete representation of life in the Middle Ages, but it is a side that we should do well to think about occasionally, and then to ask ourselves how it is that things have improved so much during a comparatively short time. It is indeed difficult to realise that so late as 1665 a great plague could devastate London as a result of the insanitary conditions; so serious was it that nearly a fifth of the population perished.

Nowadays we have roads all over the country on which we can travel without the slightest risk of robbery. In our towns we have cheap transport by trams and buses, we are provided with libraries from which we can borrow books without charge; there are swimming baths for our recreation and public parks for our enjoyment. In these days the slightest trace of a smell from drains will rouse the neighbours to action, and if anything goes wrong with the water supply, or the gas, or the electric light, there is very soon an outcry.

The transformation of the conditions of life, particularly in the towns, during the last hundred years, may be attributed to many causes. During the eighteenth century there had been much humanitarian work accomplished; men such as John Wesley and John Howard drew attention to existing conditions and roused public opinion. The sharp increase in the population—during the reign of George III it was nearly doubled—combined with the rapid industrialisation of the country, increased the problems of poverty, distress and crime. The workers themselves were at last forced to protest against the conditions under which they had to exist, and in such a movement as that of the Chartists they demanded a voice in the organisation of local affairs. Step by step the necessity for more democratic government was recognised by Parliament. The spread of education further helped to quicken men's minds to the needs of the hour. At the same time great strides were being made in the sciences, and in the art of preventive medicine, and ways of avoiding bad conditions were sought for as well as methods of curing evils.

The increasingly democratic character of the age brought with it more efficient organisation of local government, and although the system in its present form is comparatively recent, it would not be an exaggeration to say that local government in this country is older than central government. To understand this it is necessary to know something of how our present system has developed out of the past.

# THE LOCAL COMMUNITY

During the 600 years from the time the Romans left Britain until the coming of the Normans, a number of tribes invaded this country and settled down in little communities. There were different tribes of Saxons, there were Danes and Norsemen. They used a large number of different dialects, and of course brought with them their own tribal customs. One result was that the country instead of becoming one whole was split up into a number of small settlements, very loosely connected with each other. The basis of the social life was the township or village, which afterwards developed into the Parish. Probably the township, or *tun*, was at first a family settlement, and as the country had great stretches of impassable forest land and of marshes, communication between one township and another was very difficult, so that each community tended to become self-sufficient and self-governing. Where possible a number of townships sufficiently close together formed the *Hundred*, and a combination of convenient Hundreds formed the *Shire*. Many of our present counties or shires retain evidence of their tribal origin; for instance Essex was the area in which the East Saxon townships were settled. The name 'Hundred' survives in place-names, e.g. the Hundred of Hoo in Kent and the Chiltern Hundreds (see p. 109).

These various townships were probably governed by *Moots*. The head of the town's moot was known as a *Reeve*. The head of the Shire Moot was an *Ealdorman* or *Earl* (Danish, *jarl*), and the chief officer of the Shire Moot was the *Shire-reeve*, whose name still persists in our word "sheriff." He became the King's agent to see that taxes were collected; gradually his power increased.

In the course of time these various communities were adapted to changing conditions, but very little of the old system was entirely superseded, with the result that about a hundred years ago there was a confused medley of different authorities all over the country. Their powers were seldom defined by Act of Parliament but were the result of custom, and it is important that we should appreciate this factor in the development of our institutions. Custom has played a far larger part in the development of our government, both local and central, than Acts of Parliament. There has always been a curious reluctance in this country to do away with anything that has been of service in the past, so that we have had no complete breaks in our development comparable with the French and Russian Revolutions. As an illustration of this we may take the modern County High Sheriff, whose function nowadays is almost entirely decorative, but it would be against the instinct of the nation to abolish the office altogether. Here we are wise, because tradition and a sense of the past (that may seem sometimes to be carried to extremes) are the steadying factors in our developing constitutionally.

It is only during the last hundred years that local government has been co-ordinated under the central authorities. Administrative control is retained by various Government Departments, of which the most important is the Ministry of Health (formerly the Local Government Board). Control is maintained chiefly by inspection and advice, and through financial management, and very seldom by legal compulsion. The general principle of delegating responsibility (decentralisation) is preserved, and so far as practicable, local authorities are left to manage their own affairs without undue interference from the central authority, which we often call 'Whitehall', that being the place where many of the Ministries are to be found. There is a tendency to increase the powers of the county at the expense of the smaller authorities; this is a matter of convenience for administration. It is, for instance, more economical and efficient to have the roads looked after by the County Council than for a number of smaller Councils to control sections of roads; at one time the Parish was responsible for the roads, but the upkeep now is an engineering task beyond the powers of such a small unit. Some people argue that the time has come for dividing the country into a small number of large regions as this would facilitate the work involved; this might mean a gain in efficiency but it would also mean a loss of community feeling and a decline in watchfulness over local needs. Moreover such a reorganisation would cut right across county traditions. A beginning has been made in this regional system for the supply of electricity, and we may expect other schemes to follow.

## i. *Present System*

The present system of local government authorities dates from the Municipal Reform Act of 1835 and the Local Government Act of 1888 which set up the County Councils. The Local Government Act of 1933 codified the scheme. The general scheme is set out in the following table; this applies to England and Wales apart from London; we shall have to describe the system for London and for Scotland in a separate section.

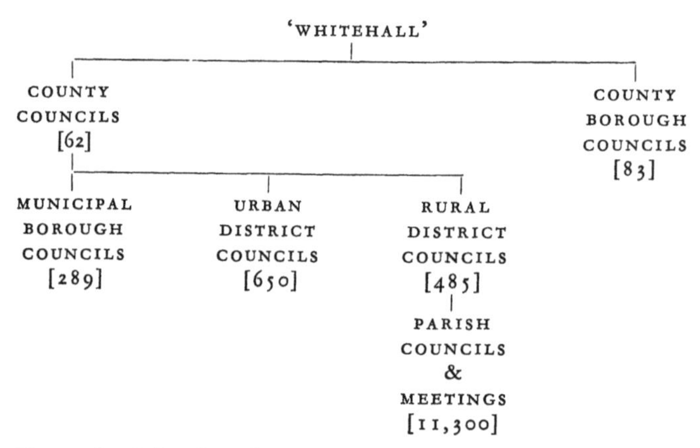


The number in brackets gives the total number of each kind of authority in England and Wales but excluding London.

We will now consider each of these Councils, its constitution, development, and authority, beginning with the Parish which has the least amount of power, and working up to the County Councils which have the greatest powers. It is not possible here to do more than select the most important of the multitude of things the Councils can do, but these should be sufficient to give a general impression of their work.

## THE PARISH

It cannot be said with any certainty how far back in our history the Parish goes. We can safely say that this division is earlier than the Norman Conquest; some believe that it was made by Theodore of Tarsus, Archbishop of Canterbury (668–92), who first formed the Parishes to ensure that each district had its priest. Up to the time of the Tudors, the Parish was mainly a part of the Church organisation, but it gradually came to be used as a convenient unit for civic purposes; for two centuries after the enactment of the Poor Law of 1601, it is no exaggeration to say that the Parish Vestry (or meeting of the parishioners) and the Justices of the Peace of the County were responsible for local government. Each Parish had to appoint Churchwardens (to see to the furnishing and upkeep of the church), Constables (see p. 50), Surveyors of the Highways (see p. 46) and Overseers of the Poor (see p. 55). The Vestry was the business meeting of the Parish; 'open' Vestries included all the parishioners; 'select' Vestries consisted of the chief householders who re-elected one another or filled vacancies. Many of the records of the parish officials and of the Vestries have been preserved and show that affairs were generally conducted with a proper sense of responsibility, though some Select Vestries misapplied the funds and considered the organisation of banquets for themselves an important part of their duties. The system broke down towards the end of the eighteenth century owing to rapid increase of population and the shifting of the main centres of work. By the Municipal Reform Act of 1835 the Parish Vestries lost much of their authority, and later changes have left the Parish Council (the legatee of the Vestry) with little to do. This Parish Council must not be confused with the Parochial Church Councils set up in 1919 as purely ecclesiastical bodies. They have nothing to do with local government.

There are 12,480 Parishes in England and Wales, but only the rural Parishes have Parish Councils or Parish Meetings. Where the population is 300 or over, an election is held every three years in May to form a Parish Council; if the population is under 300, there is usually no Council but the Parish Meeting must be held at least twice a year. The Council (or Meeting) has few powers; these are limited to such matters as allotments, footpaths, and the suppression of nuisances. The Council (Meeting) can bring to the notice of the Rural District Council or to the County Council any matters, such as housing or water supply, that need attention. There is no need for Parish Councils in towns, but in the countryside they are important links in the chain of local government since they provide every elector, even in the most thinly populated parts, with an opportunity to voice grievances or express local desires.

### DISTRICT COUNCILS

Whether a District is Urban or Rural depends on the size and degree of concentration of its population. Some Rural Districts cover enormous areas; for instance, Bellingham Rural District in Northumberland has an area of 246,645 acres, but its total population is only 5291. A more typical Rural District is Stow-on-the-Wold in Gloucestershire with an area of 44,450 acres and a population of 6284. Changes in population may necessitate adjustments of areas and of the nature of the Council; thus an increase in the population of a town owing to developments in industry may make that town the centre of an Urban District. The Local Government Boundary Commission has the authority to recommend changes to meet new conditions.

District Councils consist of Councillors elected for a period of three years, one-third of them retiring each year but being eligible for re-election. They appoint a Chairman from amongst themselves. Urban District Councils have rather more power than Rural Councils; both are concerned with such matters as sanitary services, lighting, control of building, water supply, and food inspection. The tendency, however, is for more and more of these functions to be controlled by the County Council with the District Councils acting as agents. The importance of these local Councils lies not so much in their authority to do things, as in their being 'on the spot', and so making it possible for the inhabitants to bring to the notice of the Councillors living amongst them, any matters that call for attention.

### MUNICIPAL BOROUGHS

It will be seen in the above table that there are now two kinds of Borough—the Municipal and the County. Like the Parish, the Borough has a long history behind it. Trade had much to do with the rise of the Boroughs; the merchants in a market town were important citizens in the Middle Ages, and they were able to bargain for privileges from the King or from an overlord for the control of the town affairs. If the King or the overlord was in need of money he might be willing to grant a Charter giving a town considerable rights in managing its own government; so the town became a Borough with a large degree of independence in exchange for substantial aid to the King or overlord. The withdrawal of a Charter could be a serious set-back to a town; this method of putting pressure on a Borough was used by Charles II and James II, but after 1688 those Boroughs that had been deprived of their rights had their old Charters restored to them.

Boroughs were governed by a Corporation consisting of a Mayor with a number of Aldermen and Councillors. Many of these Corporations became shamefully corrupt before the nineteenth century; some were like private clubs uncontrolled by free electors or by a central authority. This was one of the reasons for the great Municipal Reform Act of 1835. The Mayor and Aldermen are now elected by the Councillors who themselves are elected by qualified citizens. The Mayor serves for one year but can be reappointed; in large cities he has the title of Lord Mayor. Aldermen serve for six years and the Councillors for three years; one-third of the Councillors retire each year but are eligible for re-election.

As a result of their varied origins, the Boroughs differ considerably in population; some ancient Boroughs have smaller populations than some towns that are not Boroughs. For instance, Tewkesbury in Gloucestershire received its charter from Queen Elizabeth in 1576, and although its population is only 4400 it is still a Borough.

New Boroughs can be created by Royal Charter out of towns that so far have been the centres of Urban Districts. It is a great day for a town when it receives its Charter for the first time and sees its Mayor in his new robes and wearing a chain of office, the Aldermen and Councillors in their gowns, and the be-wigged Town Clerk. Such outward signs of office have importance in promoting civic pride and a desire amongst the inhabitants to make their town the finest in the country.

## COUNTY BOROUGHS

County Boroughs, as distinct from Municipal Boroughs, were created by the Local Government Act of 1888. The status was granted to towns in England and Wales having populations of at least 50,000. It was felt that towns of this size were large enough to provide themselves with the services the public expects, such as schools, police, and so on. They are thus independent to a large degree of the County Councils. Thus you may find that the town where the County Council meets (often in the Shire Hall) is itself a County Borough; Reading, for example, with a population of over 108,000, is both a County Borough and the meeting place of the Berkshire County Council. Since 1888 a number of towns have been raised to the rank of County Borough, but since 1926 a minimum population of 75,000 has been required. It would now probably have to be 100,000 to justify such a change of status.

There are many advantages in being a County Borough; the people on the spot are in charge of their affairs and have not to go to the County Council, cap in hand, to get improvements they may be anxious to gain. A County Council is never willing for any town within its boundaries to become a County Borough; it naturally feels that it means a loss of power, and it certainly means a loss of revenue; so any proposal of this kind, or from an existing County Borough to extend its boundaries, meets with strong opposition. An imaginary case will illustrate the problem. Let us suppose that on the outskirts of the County Borough of Lumbury there is a rapidly growing residential area we will call Rubicon. Perhaps the development of a new industry has resulted in an increased population for Lumbury and the newcomers have to be provided with houses. The only available area for this is in Rubicon Rural District. These newcomers have no traditional ties with Rubicon and they are not pleased to find that the services to which they are accustomed, such as sanitation and lighting and transport, cannot be provided by a Rural District on account of the great expense involved. So they agitate for their new district to be brought within the boundaries of Lumbury which, as a County Borough, can do all they need. The old inhabitants of Rubicon may object strongly —they prefer to be a quiet rural area rather than an offshoot of a town. The County may object to the proposed extension as it means a loss of income for the County. These various opinions are not easily reconciled and it may take long negotiations and a public inquiry before the Local Government Boundary Commission makes a decision.

The powers of a County Borough are in the main similar to those of a County Council, so it will be simpler to deal with these under the next heading.

### COUNTY COUNCILS

The County is an ancient division of the country that goes back to the Shire of Saxon times. Not much is known about the origins of most of the Shires; those in southern England can be traced back to an earlier period than most of the others; this is due to the chance that more records, such as the *Anglo-Saxon Chronicle*, have survived relating to this region than for the more northerly parts. The Shires may have been areas of conquest, or divisions made by kings and put under the control of earls. It was after the Conquest that the Shires were made the judicial and administrative units for the country. It then became necessary to mark boundaries more precisely, especially in the north. The last County to be established was Lancashire in the twelfth century.

A map of Tudor England and Wales gives forty Counties in England and twelve in Wales. These are still the geographical Counties, but for local government purposes some are divided into two or more administrative Counties; some of these are ancient regions. For example, Lincolnshire is divided into the Parts of Holland, Kesteven, and Lindsey; Suffolk and Sussex are each divided into East and West, while in Yorkshire there are the three Ridings ('thirdings')—East, North, and West. London was made a separate County in 1888 (not a County borough). So there are sixty-two administrative counties in England and Wales.

It is an interesting task to find out all we can about the history of our own county; some puzzling questions may arise; for instance, why have detached bits of Worcestershire been left like islands inside neighbouring Counties? The position of county boundaries brings up a number of interesting problems, and in trying to solve these we shall find ourselves going back into the days of early England, and we shall realise that our Counties and Boroughs have long traditions behind them.

If we could start with a blank map we should, no doubt, produce a much tidier plan, but it would lack much of the interest of the irregular divisions we have inherited. A New Town can be laid out with all modern conveniences and be suited to the needs of motor traffic; but it must lack the warmth and romance of the towns that are summaries, as we may call them, of our past, with their buildings of several centuries and their crooked and often narrow streets that still follow the medieval ways.

Counties and County Boroughs have considerable powers of self-government. Most of these are derived from Acts of Parliament, and there are some 'Adoptive' Acts which allow local authorities to do things if they so desire. For instance they can spend money on public libraries if they want to, but they are not compelled to do so. Some services are so important, such as education and health, that they must be provided. It will be sufficient here to mention a few of the most important duties of the County Councils—control of building, slum clearance, schools, inspection of food, parks, police, sanitation, roads.

The County Council consists of a Chairman and Vice-Chairman (a County Borough will have a Mayor), with Aldermen and Councillors. All the Councillors are elected as a body every three years (not as in Municipal Boroughs), but only half the Aldermen have to be elected by the Councillors after the County Council Election has been held.

## ii. *An Example*

Now that we have surveyed the kinds of Council, it will be of interest to see how the scheme applies to one county—Berkshire. The sketch-map includes the Parliamentary boundaries, but we are not at present concerned with these (see pp. 109–110). The Parishes are not given as these are too many to be included on a small-scale map.

Berkshire is a good example of irregular shape; the northern boundary is a natural one, being determined by the windings of the River Thames.

There are eleven Rural Districts, the smallest of which is Windsor with an area of just under 9000 acres and a population of about 10,000; the largest Rural District is Abingdon with 42,000 acres and just over 12,000 inhabitants. There is only one Urban District—Wantage, with a population of less than 4000. Most Counties have more than one Urban District; Surrey, for instance, has twenty-three. There are six Municipal Boroughs in Berkshire, and, as the following list shows, they vary considerably in populations:

| | |
|---|---|
| Wallingford | 3,418 |
| Wokingham | 8,445 |
| Abingdon | 10,900 |
| Newbury | 17,680 |
| Windsor | 21,710 |
| Maidenhead | 26,790 |

The explanation of this diversity will be found in the histories of these towns. You will find it interesting to look up the date when each town received its Charter; thus Wallingford has been a Borough since the time of Edward the Confessor.

Reading is the only County Borough in Berkshire. Some Counties have several County Boroughs; Lancashire, for instance, has as many as fifteen, while others, such as Hertfordshire, have none.

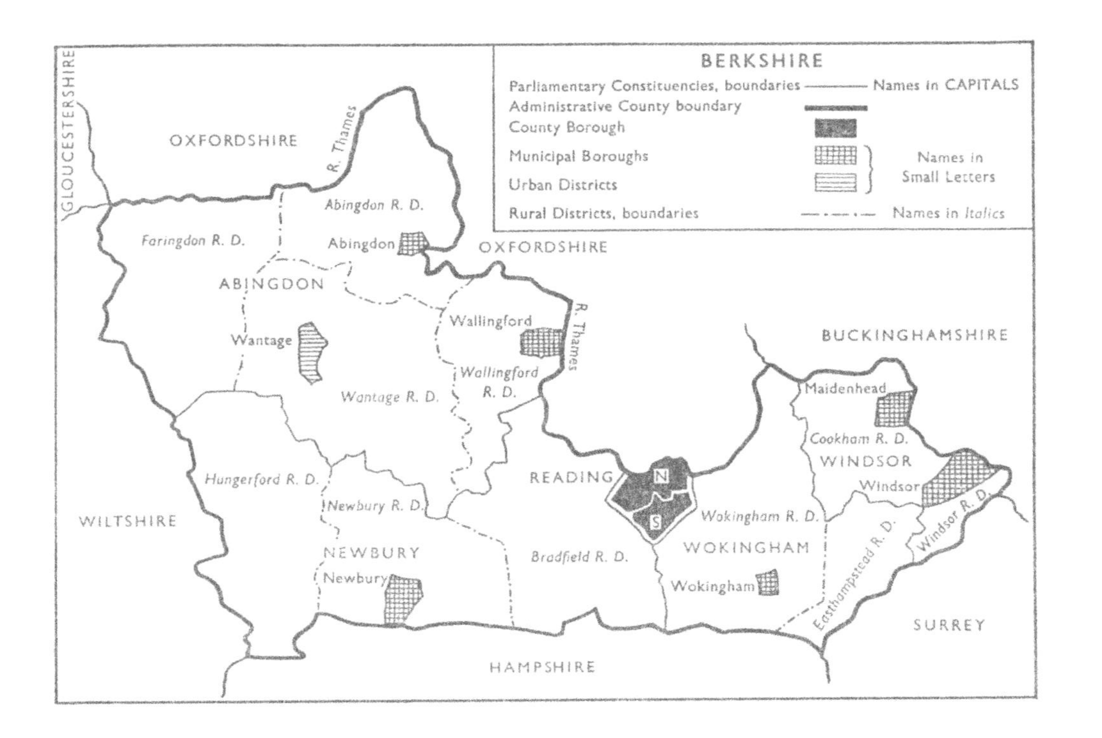
BERKSHIRE
Parliamentary Constituencies, boundaries — Names in CAPITALS
Administrative County boundary
County Borough
Municipal Boroughs
Urban Districts
Names in Small Letters
Rural Districts, boundaries — Names in Italics
GLOUCESTERSHIRE
OXFORDSHIRE
R. Thames
Abingdon R. D.
Faringdon R. D.
Abingdon
OXFORDSHIRE
ABINGDON
Wantage
Wallingford
R. Thames
BUCKINGHAMSHIRE
Wallingford R. D.
Wantage R. D.
Maidenhead
Cookham R. D.
WINDSOR
Hungerford R. D.
READING
N
S
Windsor
Newbury R. D.
Wokingham R. D.
WILTSHIRE
Easthampstead R. D.
Windsor R. D.
NEWBURY
Bradfield R. D.
WOKINGHAM
Newbury
Wokingham
SURREY
HAMPSHIRE

You will have noticed that a name may be repeated two or three times; thus 'Abingdon' may apply to the town or Borough, to the Rural District, or to the Parliamentary Constituency.

If you do not live in Berkshire, make a similar sketch map for your County, and look up the history of each Borough.

## iii. *How a Council Works*

The short accounts given above of the powers of the various Councils show that they have a great deal to do; County Councils and County Borough Councils have the most to do. How do they organise their work?

It would be impracticable for every detail to be discussed in full Council. There are, for instance, on the Gloucestershire County Council, 21 Aldermen and 65 Councillors; if 86 people get together to discuss business they must of necessity limit the number of topics to be dealt with; should they attempt to discuss every point connected with the Council's work, they would exhaust their time and themselves. It should never be forgotten that all Councillors are voluntary workers; some may be men or women of leisure, but most have to give some attention to their own affairs. One criticism of our present system is that full-time workers cannot undertake the responsibilities of being County Councillors; they can more easily be members of District Councils that may meet in the evenings; but it would be impossible for County Councils and County Borough Councils and for many large Municipal Councils to transact all the business in evening meetings, so the tendency is for County Councillors to be retired men or married women or those who have done well enough in their professions or businesses to be able to attend meetings during the daytime. This is an undoubted weakness. It has been suggested that Councillors should be paid like Members of Parliament, but there is a natural reluctance to break the long tradition of voluntary service. The problem may become more acute with the increasing burden of work being put on County Councils. It is clearly most desirable that our Councillors should be men and women of intelligence and experience and young enough to stand the strain of the work.

The work is organised under Committees. Each of these deals with one part of the work and presents a report, usually monthly, to the full Council. In this way much time is saved as the Committees investigate and discuss the details of problems and plans, and the full Council can then concentrate on major matters of policy. This does not mean that the full Council never discusses details; a Councillor may feel that the Committee has overlooked some important point; but the Council is usually content to accept the material for discussion as set out in the Committee report and then itself to consider the recommendations made in it.

Here are some of the Committees of a County Council.

| | |
|---|---|
| Agriculture | Highways |
| Education | Housing |
| Finance | Planning |
| Health | |

Each of these may have Sub-Committees; for instance the Education Committee has Sub-Committees for agricultural education, higher education, libraries, primary education, and technical education. Sometimes men and women who are not Councillors are co-opted on to these Committees and Sub-Committees; they usually have special knowledge or experience that is valuable.

As far as possible a Councillor is appointed to those Committees where his own interests lie; if, for instance, he is interested in schools, he will probably be put on the Education Committee. In this way the best use is made of a Councillor's enthusiasm and knowledge.

CHAPTER IV

# WHAT IS DONE LOCALLY

A long book would be needed to describe all the work carried out by the Councils; in this chapter we shall limit our survey to (i) Education, (ii) Public Health, (iii) Roads, and (iv) Police.

## i. *Education*

Few things are more confusing to a foreigner visiting this country than the rather complicated system of names that we have for our different kinds of schools. At first sight there appears to be no system at all; but our organisation of education is, like so many other of our institutions, the result of long growth and development and carries with it still many signs and memories of that past history. We are gradually developing an orderly system.

We are so accustomed to think that it is the business of the State to provide for the education of its citizens that we sometimes do not realise how comparatively modern is this idea. Before the nineteenth century there was no popular education in the present sense of the term. There have been schools since the time of Alfred, some endowed by individuals or by a Gild, others attached to churches. Many schools were founded, or re-founded, in the reigns of Edward VI and Elizabeth on funds derived from confiscated church endowments, but these schools were very unevenly distributed and only affected a small proportion of the population.

A typical school of the Tudor period was the Grammar School at Stratford-on-Avon to which Shakespeare went. There the main subject of instruction was Latin, hence the name 'Grammar'. If a boy showed promise he might at the age of fifteen go on to a university. So far as we know

Shakespeare left school at an earlier age than that and possibly entered his father's business. London was better provided with schools at the time of the Tudors than any other town in the kingdom, but by the eighteenth century schools everywhere had fallen in efficiency and the education given was very poor.

One of the most valued forms of elementary education was begun towards the end of the eighteenth century with the Sunday School movement. The first object of this was religious instruction and the children were taught to read the Bible; the memorising of the catechism, of passages from the Bible and of hymns constituted the greater part of the work. Writing and arithmetic were taught in a few, but this type of education was naturally limited and could not be very effective as the majority of the children from the age of six or seven were in active employment, and might be working for many hours a day.

The next important step was taken early in the nineteenth century by two societies, the National Society for Promoting the Education of the Poor in the Principles of the Established Church, and the British and Foreign School Society. These founded elementary schools maintained by means of subscriptions and small fees. The first step in State control was taken in 1833, when Parliament made an annual grant of £20,000 towards the building of schools by these two societies. This amount was increased gradually and in 1858 amounted to £663,000. It is interesting to compare this figure with the sum of £189,020,000 spent during 1948 under the Education Acts in England and Wales.

The voluntary method of providing popular education was found to be inadequate. In 1860, for instance, few children were educated at all after the age of eleven, and generally they spent less than 100 days a year in school. The first big step forward was taken in 1870 when the Elementary Education Act was passed. This provided for the setting up and maintaining at the public expense of schools wherever provision at that date was inadequate. School Boards were set up with power to levy a local rate for educational purposes. At first it was impossible to make attendance compulsory, simply because there were neither sufficient schools nor teachers, but as time went on and the accommodation became sufficient the age of leaving was raised from ten to eleven in 1893, to twelve in 1899 and to fourteen in 1900. The Act of 1944 raised the age to fifteen as soon as conditions would make it practicable, with the prospect of a further rise to sixteen.

In 1899 the Board of Education was set up; it replaced the Committee of Council which had controlled grants. The Board was given the power of inspecting schools and of administering the funds provided by the State. In 1944 the 'Board' became the 'Ministry' of Education, and the 'President' of the old Board was renamed 'Minister of Education'. This may seem a slight change, but the 'Board' had for long been a fiction, and it was desired to mark the importance of the position of the member of the Government in charge of educational affairs.

The Education Act of 1944 reorganised the system of national education. The County and County Borough Councils were made responsible for putting the scheme into operation. Previously many Borough Councils and some Urban District Councils had control over public elementary schools; they can now act as agents of the County Councils and so retain their local interest in the schools.

The Councils are not responsible for arranging the time-tables, nor for issuing instructions on how subjects shall be taught. These are matters for the teachers to decide. Nor does the Ministry of Education issue such instructions, nor does it issue text-books or prescribe what text-books shall be used. By its Inspectors, the Ministry makes sure that the standard of teaching is satisfactory and that the general lines of education are in keeping with the broad policy laid down. It gives advice to Councils and to teachers through these

Inspectors and by the publication of pamphlets and in other ways keeps them informed of new ideas and methods. The Councils provide the buildings and the necessary equipment and see that schools are properly staffed.

Parents are by law responsible for seeing that their children receive efficient full-time education from the age of five until the school-leaving age. The children need not go to the schools provided by the Councils; home-tuition or attendance at private schools is permissible provided it is considered of a satisfactory character. Many private schools (including some known as the Public Schools) receive financial aid from public funds; others are inspected and recognised as efficient but are self-supporting through endowments and fees. The 1944 Act provided for the inspection of all schools, so that no one in future will be able to start a school unless certain standards of teachers' qualifications and of building and equipment are reached. Actually 91·5 per cent of the children in England and Wales in 1947 between the ages of five and fourteen attended schools either maintained entirely or aided partly by public funds. Or, to put it another way, even where parents pay high fees for private schools, part of the total cost may be covered by public funds. No fees are charged in any schools maintained by the Councils.

Children between the ages of two and five years may attend Nursery Schools or Classes. This is a comparatively recent development; its value was found during the 1939–45 war when mothers were employed in factories or engaged in some kind of war-work. The 1944 Act makes it part of the Councils' work to provide such schools where there is the need for them.

Compulsory schooling begins at the age of five. The Primary School stage lasts until the pupils are between eleven and twelve years of age; this period of a year allows for varying rates of development, but the normal age of change is nearer eleven years than twelve. This stage is divided into two; the Infant School up to the age of seven or eight, and sometimes even older, followed by the Junior School. At the change-over period of eleven to twelve, the boy or girl passes to a Secondary School.

There are three kinds of Secondary School:

(1) The Grammar School,
(2) The Modern School, and
(3) The Technical School.

Why should there be these three kinds? Why not a common Secondary School for all? The explanation is that boys and girls vary in their abilities and tastes. To force all through the same kind of training would mean that many would waste their time trying to learn things or do things for which they have no capacity. This is not only a hardship to them, but it is a loss to the community which can benefit from the full development of each member's abilities. It would be possible to devise a large number of different types of school to meet many kinds of need, but this broad classification of three types goes some way to solve the problem; it should be remembered that within each kind of school there is also some choice of subjects.

(1) *The Grammar School* continues the kind of work we have been accustomed to associate with Secondary Schools (including the ancient Grammar Schools): English, a foreign language and sometimes Latin, geography, history, mathematics and science.

(2) *The Modern School* provides education for the majority of boys and girls. In addition to ordinary subjects there is a wide range of crafts and practical subjects.

(3) *The Technical School* pays special attention to those who show aptitude for industry and commerce, and appeals to those whose bent is towards the practical and the constructive.

Grammar Schools aim at keeping most of their pupils until the age of seventeen or eighteen; some will then go on to the Universities or to some other form of advanced education.

In the other Secondary Schools the pupils can remain until the age of sixteen; some of them may go on to other institutions for further training.

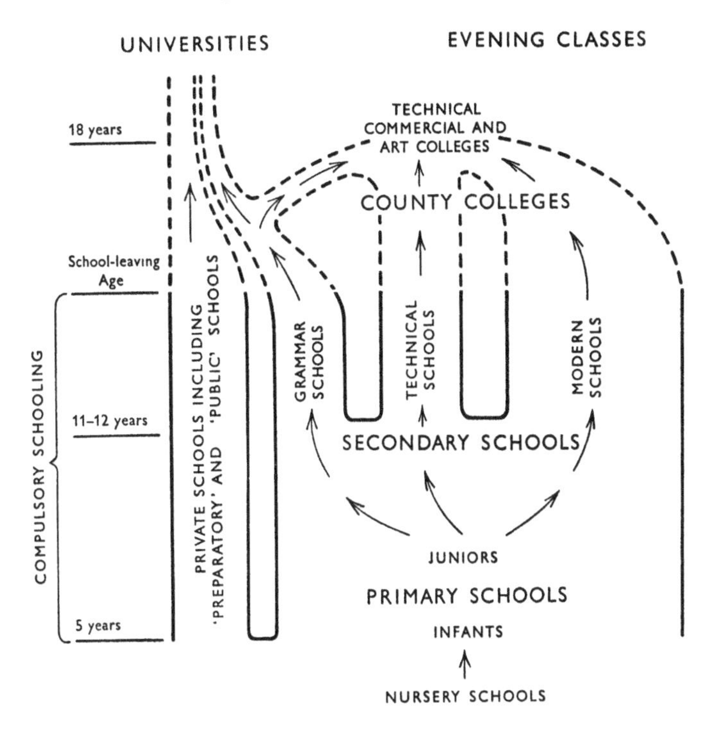


The main difference between one type of Secondary School and another is not a matter of social standing; it is all a question of trying to fit each boy or girl into the kind of school best suited to his or her abilities.

It will be realised how important is the decision taken at the age of eleven to twelve for the future of any boy or girl. Various methods are employed in making this decision—

written examinations, interviews, and the opinions of the teachers under whom the child has worked, all are used in selecting the kind of Secondary School to which he or she goes after leaving the Primary School. Even so, mistakes can be made; some children develop more slowly than others and unsuspected abilities may be revealed after the age of twelve years. It has therefore been arranged that another consideration of the question can be taken, if felt desirable, at the age of thirteen, and a transfer made from one type of Secondary School to another.

The Councils are also responsible for establishing other kinds of school. They can, for instance, provide Boarding Schools or pay the fees for boys and girls to go to existing Boarding Schools. Then there are the needs of handicapped children to be considered—the blind, the deaf, or those suffering from other physical or mental disabilities that prevent them from going to ordinary schools. For these unfortunates special schools can be provided.

This does not complete the picture of our national system of education. An important innovation under the Act of 1944 was the proposal to form County Colleges. Boys and girls who leave school at fifteen or sixteen years of age must attend these Colleges for one day a week during forty-four weeks in a year until they reach the age of eighteen.

The Councils are also responsible for providing many kinds of voluntary training for adults by means of evening classes and lectures. Nor should we forget the importance of libraries, museums, civic theatres and concerts as part of our educational opportunities.

It would not be too much to say that the educational work of our Councils is their most important undertaking and the Committees who have this work in their care are rendering a great service to the community.

## ii. *Public Health*

The need for proper sanitation and for the creation of healthy conditions of living is now recognised by all of us, but it has taken a long time and much bitter experience for the lesson to be learned. Scientists have taught us that good health is directly connected with cleanliness of our towns, with pure water and with good houses. We have inherited bad as well as good things; amongst the bad must be included narrow streets of poky houses in continuous rows and built back to back. The lack of sufficient houses has resulted in overcrowding. It takes a long time for such evils to be banished. The air-raids during the 1939–45 war increased the problem enormously. Bad sanitation and bad housing mean bad health; let us therefore glance at these two aspects of Public Health and see what the local Councils can do about them to effect improvements.

Have you ever realised what a lot of waste materials have somehow or other to be disposed of? We put our rubbish into a dustbin, we pour our slops down a drain and think nothing much of it, and yet such things as drains and sewers and the destruction of rubbish have a comparatively recent history. It is astonishing really that there was not more disease in pre-sanitary days than there was, for refuse and sewage were allowed to contaminate streams and rivers and so bring about various diseases such as diphtheria and typhoid fever. The smallness of the population before 1800 was a saving factor: the open country was never far away. We have now, thanks to the work of our local authorities, an excellent system of drainage and sewage. In London alone, for instance, there are nearly 2500 miles of sewers, and it is estimated that every day about 250,000,000 gallons of sewage flow to the outfalls. This has to be dealt with by various means and the sewage taken away and deposited in some safe place where it cannot be a nuisance. In London it is pumped into special vessels and then taken out into the North Sea and deposited. To a less degree the same necessity applies to all districts, and we should very soon realise, not merely by objectionable smells, but by an increase in disease, if the important duty of providing sound drains and sewers were not being carried out by the authorities.

Sanitary environment also includes the provision of a pure water supply. Pollution of wells and other sources of drinking water is bound to lead to disease, and happily we have now in this country an excellent supply of drinking water in many areas, though some rural districts still have to rely on wells or rain-water. Reservoirs have been constructed as far as possible up in the hills, from which a sound supply of water can be obtained. It is hardly necessary to point out that a sanitary supply of water is an important element in health, and it makes cleanliness easier, not only for the person but for the house.

Another important element in the sanitary environment is housing. We have heard a good deal about this subject of recent years, partly on account of the house shortage since the war, due not only to destruction in air-raids but to the cessation of building during the war period. The far more important problem arises of providing sound living conditions for everybody. The worst aspect of the problem is that of the slums in many of our large towns, and much has already been done to remedy this evil. The larger authorities have cleared out some of the terrible slums and built in their place pleasant streets of houses or blocks of flats with wide roads and facilities for playgrounds and for pleasant living, but much still remains to be done, and in this direction the ordinary citizen can do good service by getting to know the facts about housing in his own locality and by urging the local authorities to exercise the powers which they have by Act of Parliament. These powers include:

1. The building of houses on land acquired or appropriated.

2. The rebuilding of any houses or tenements that do not come up to the minimum requirements for healthy living.

3. Power to lay out and construct streets in such a way that the maximum amount of open space can be obtained.

4. The power to issue closing orders if the house is considered unfit for human habitation, and demolition orders if such a house has not been made fit within six months.

These powers are fairly wide, and in fact if any local authority seriously means to improve the housing within its area, it can do so. This often, of course, means overcoming vested interests, and this can only be done where the local authority is backed up by a strong public opinion.

The housing problem, however, is not merely concerned with present conditions but with future possibilities. Towns have grown up in a haphazard sort of way and have gradually spread themselves over the surrounding countryside, very much according to the wishes and whims of the builder. It is now possible by means of the various Town Planning Acts for a local authority to control all building within its area. It can plan out roads, it can decide how much land is needed for each house, it can ensure proper sanitary conditions and can also provide for open spaces and other amenities. Here there is a large field for good work, so that gradually in the course of time our towns as they grow will not disfigure the countryside, and the houses will be healthy and pleasant.

The Ministry of Town and Country Planning has considerable powers of control over all developments. New Towns have been planned to draw off some of the population from congested cities.

## iii. *Roads*

Effective road legislation begins in the year 1555 when an Act was passed for the organisation of the maintenance of highways. The main principles of that Act remained in force for nearly 300 years. The obligation to maintain the roads was put upon the Parish, which had to appoint a Surveyor of Highways. This latter appointment was by no means a pleasant one, for all the manual labour, including the tools required for the work, had to be provided gratuitously by the inhabitants and the surveyor had to persuade them to do their share of the work. Anyone could supply another labourer in place of himself if he wished to do so. This system was certainly better than nothing at all, but it really effected very little, for everyone strove to evade the duty of providing highway labour and a man was quite willing to connive at his neighbour doing the same for the sake of his own peace.

Moreover very little was known about the science of road-making; the method employed was to level off the track very roughly and to fill in the numerous holes and pits with gravel or even earth. Each winter, or even one bad storm, destroyed the work done.

The position began to get serious during the seventeenth century with the increase of traffic. It must be remembered that even up to the eighteenth century wheeled traffic was very rare. Most travellers went on horseback. But by this time London was demanding more goods from the country, trade was opening up everywhere and it was soon found that the miry tracks which had served as roads for so many centuries were no longer equal to the demands of the traffic. Later came the stage coaches and the institution of a regular postal service, and soon it was realised that the efficiency of these was very much impaired by the appalling conditions of the so-called roads. So fresh means of improving them had to be devised. The Parishes were no longer equal to the task. The outcome of this position was not the creation of any kind of central organisation but the creation of Turnpike Trusts. Each Trust was established by Act of Parliament and thousands of these Acts were passed from 1706 onwards.

A Trust consisted of local people of position who were empowered to construct and maintain a definite stretch of road and to levy tolls towards the cost of maintenance. This system was adopted throughout the country and soon Turnpike Roads with their toll-gates came into existence. The system, however, was open to many abuses. It was very soon realised that here was a source of income for the Turnpike Trustees, which could be used not primarily for maintaining the road but for personal profit. Moreover the increasing number of toll-gates added considerably to the cost of travel. Some idea of this may be gathered from the fact that the turnpike at Chalk in Kent was let for £300 a year, and one gate on the Brighton road was said to have taken £2400 a year in tolls.

The opening of the nineteenth century was the beginning of a new era for roads and the first step was taken by the General Post Office, owing to the demand for a speedier service between London and Dublin, via Holyhead. The Post Office had for some time tried to stir up the local Turnpike Trusts to carry out their duties, but unsuccessfully. The matter by now, however, had been taken up by the House of Commons, and the famous Thomas Telford (1757–1834) was employed to reconstruct the road from London to Holyhead. This set a standard of achievement which was only equalled by the work of John McAdam (1756–1836), a man of independent means with a passion for everything connected with roads. His name survives in that given to one particular type of construction, 'the macadamised highway'. The Turnpike Trusts still existed and the first blow at their prosperity came with the introduction of the railways between 1830 and 1850, and for over half a century some of them continued to struggle on. In 1864 the House of Commons formed a committee to inquire into the working of the Turnpike Trusts and decided that their abolition was expedient. The last of all came to an end in 1895—the Turnpike Trust for part of the Holyhead road in Anglesey.

This gradual transference of thousands of miles of roads which had been under the Turnpike Trusts to the Parishes naturally caused some dismay as it considerably increased local expenses. Grants were made by Parliament to ease the situation, and in 1888 the duty of maintenance of main roads was transferred from the parishes to the County Councils. Roads are still administered within Boroughs or Urban Districts by the Town or District Council, and outside these areas the main roads are maintained by the County Council.

The twentieth century meant the coming of the motor-car. Even the bicycle had made roads more popular, and it is amusing to read in the papers of the eighties and nineties of last century of complaints about the alarm the bicyclist caused to pedestrians, the dust he raised or mud he splashed up, and the recklessness of his riding; but the humble bicycle could not compare with the motor-car for making the question of road maintenance an urgent one, and it was felt that it could not remain a local question as the people who used the roads came from many different areas. Relief to the ratepayer came, however, in 1909, when taxes were put upon petrol and licence duties imposed on cars for the purpose of providing money for the maintenance of the roads. This sum formed the Road Fund, administered by the Minister of Transport, but the Fund is now no longer dependent on licence fees; the grants are paid out of the National Exchequer as for other purposes.

Since 1937 the Ministry of Transport has been responsible for the maintenance of the great main roads called Trunk Roads; the total length of these in 1947 was 8190 miles out of a total of 183,086 miles for all roads.

The subject of roads cannot be left without saying something about the accidents and deaths that are a matter of serious concern to all of us. In Great Britain during 1947 the number of people injured in road accidents was 161,318; in addition 4881 were killed. The corresponding figures for 1937 were 226,402 and 6633. It is to be hoped that this improvement is due to greater care taken by pedestrians and by motorists; but the decrease is partly due to the smaller number of vehicles on the road and to the restrictions of petrol rationing.

For our guidance we have the Highway Code, described as "a set of commonsense provisions for the guidance and safety of all who use the roads". Each of us should know that Code thoroughly and follow its wise advice.

## iv. *Police*

Whenever we refer to 'Bobbies' or 'Peelers' we are paying a compliment to Sir Robert Peel, who founded the first Police Force in London in 1829. These policemen, or constables, were dressed in cutaway blue coats, white trousers and top-hats. They were armed with batons only. Since their first appearance in the streets of London we have grown so accustomed to the efficient way in which they carry out their duties that we sometimes forget the tremendous change that the formation of the Police Force meant to the country. Up to that time there had been no satisfactory method of keeping law and order. In times of riot it was necessary to call out the military to deal with any serious situation. This resulted in such terrible affairs as the Peterloo Massacre, when a large crowd was dispersed by the soldiers in Manchester during August 1819. On that occasion eleven people were killed and some 600 wounded. Readers of Dickens' *Barnaby Rudge* will remember incidents he gives there from the Lord George Gordon Riots in 1780, when some 50,000 people marched to the House of Commons to demand the repeal of the Catholic Relief Act. During the riots over 200 were killed by the soldiers and a large number wounded and arrested. Such scenes as these are almost inconceivable now because we have grown accustomed to the idea that the police will maintain order without the use of firearms.

Centuries ago the responsibility for keeping order was placed upon each Hundred, and everyone was in a sense a constable. Even to-day all citizens are liable to be called upon to render aid as constables, and on occasion some of them are enrolled as special constables for emergencies which are too great for the normal police strength. Before police forces were organised, each Parish appointed its constable whose sign of office was a staff sometimes fastened to the door of his house to proclaim his authority. Shakespeare made fun of the constable in Dogberry (*Much Ado*), and he was indeed often a harmless person whom no one took seriously.

Many towns had a night-watchman, who carried a lantern and a large rattle. He paraded the streets of the town during the night and cried out the hour and the state of the weather—"Eleven o'clock and a fine night". This seems to have been very reassuring to our ancestors. He was, however, in no position to deal effectively with rogues and vagabonds, for the streets he walked were mostly unlighted and he had to rely entirely on his own resources for dealing with thieves and other marauders. Sometimes the ineffective official watchmen were supplemented by others employed privately by such corporations as Insurance Societies. You will still see, fixed on the front walls of some old houses, the badge of such a society; this was to notify their watchman to keep a special eye on such houses.

How inadequate policing was at the beginning of the nineteenth century may be judged from the fact that Portsmouth had twenty-two officers to protect a population of 50,000, and Liverpool had fifty watchmen to maintain order amongst 240,000 people.

The success of Sir Robert Peel's Police Act for London was so soon evident that the system was extended to the rest of the country, and in 1835 every borough had to have a police force.

In some ways our police system is unique. It is a civilian, not a military force. Much of its prestige is due to this important fact, for if the maintenance of law and order were to depend on the argument of swords and revolvers, we should very soon cease to respect our police, but rather regard them as our enemies. The baton or truncheon that a policeman carries is rarely used and is not even visible. The phrase "Ask a policeman" has become proverbial as a result of the tradition of courtesy and of helpfulness built up during the last hundred years. So friendly are our relationships with them that we seldom realise what extensive powers they have. They can of course arrest anyone seen breaking the law, but they may also arrest on suspicion if they think a breach of the peace is about to be committed. The police also provide for the public safety by controlling the use of explosives and firearms, and by insisting on proper precautions to prevent fire. They control street trading, keep a register of aliens, and suppress street betting.

Various other duties besides maintenance of the King's Peace have fallen to the police owing to force of circumstances. Of these the most pressing is the regulation of traffic. Indeed this would seem at first sight to be the most important of their duties at present, and it makes such a demand on their numbers that increases in the force are necessary, so that the patrolling of streets and demands in emergencies may not be neglected.

During this century the police forces have made use of every possible invention, such as radio, to add to their efficiency.

With the exception of the Metropolitan Police (see p. 67) the organisation of the various forces is in the hands of the local authorities. The head officer of a County or Borough Force is the Chief Constable, whose appointment must be approved by the Home Office. Further supervision by the central authority is exercised through the Inspectors of Constabulary, and, if their reports are satisfactory, the Police Grant towards local expenses is made. Throughout most of the country the police are organised on a county basis and are controlled by a joint committee, generally known as the Watch Committee, consisting of magistrates and nominees of the County Council. The county police area does not include all Boroughs, for any Borough which had a population of more than 10,000 in 1881, or in the case of a new Borough a population of 20,000, may have its own police force under a local Watch Committee; but most Boroughs now prefer to merge these powers into those of the county.

Police forces in 1947:

| | | |
|---|---|---|
| England and Wales: | Men | 55,078 |
| | Women | 896 |
| Scotland | Men | 6,742 |
| | Women | 102 |
| Total cost, Great Britain: | | £38,775,000 |

## CHAPTER V

# SOCIAL SECURITY

All communities have to face the necessity of helping the destitute. Men and women have been haunted by the fear of sickness that may prevent them from maintaining themselves and their families, or of losing their jobs and becoming destitute. There is the fear too of becoming dependent on others in old age. Past efforts to deal with such situations have usually been of a local character—personal charity (in the proper sense of the word), the Church, the Parish, or the Council. This help, whatever its inadequacies, was at least a practical possibility when the population of the country was small compared with that of modern times. In 1547 there were, perhaps, as many as four million people in England and Wales; in 1947 there were over forty-three millions. It has therefore become necessary for a greater centralisation of any system of help; the County and County Borough Councils still have important work to do in health (as distinct from public health) but such matters as unemployment insurance, and old age pensions, are organised nationally rather than locally. It will, however, be best to consider all these questions of social security in one chapter rather than postpone part until we are dealing with national affairs.

## i. *Poverty*

There is an old nursery rhyme which begins "Hark! Hark! The dogs do bark, the beggars are coming to town". This is a relic from the days when able-bodied rogues and vagabonds were becoming a real menace to the public peace. The news that a company of beggars was approaching a village would send the inhabitants indoors, and they would bolt and bar their doors as if a foreign army were approaching.

This state of affairs was at its worst during the early part of the sixteenth century. There were a number of causes to account for the sudden increase in vagabondage. The end of the long period of wars during the fifteenth century set free many who had previously found occupation as soldiers. They were men who had become accustomed to taking life and booty and consequently thought nothing of molesting ordinary people. They were the "Rogues in buckram" that Shakespeare shows us in the Falstaff scenes of *Henry IV*. A more far-reaching cause, however, was the gradual change which had come over the country during the fifteenth century. A merchant class had arisen and trade, especially in cloth, was becoming more lucrative than agriculture. Sheep rearing became more profitable than the growing of corn; consequently many thousands of acres which had hitherto been put to the plough were now put down to pasture, and great numbers of ploughmen and other farm labourers were left without employment. These men had no alternative but to wander about the country begging their bread wherever they could, and sometimes, in their necessity, taking to theft and violence. The problem became more urgent owing to the fact that with the dissolution of the monasteries one means of assistance was cut off. Most of the monasteries, though not all, had done their best to provide food and occasional lodging for any who applied at their doors, but in the best of their days they were quite unable to cope with the enormous increase in the number of beggars and vagabonds.

Those who were members of one of the Trade Gilds were looked after during times of sickness and bad trade by the Gilds themselves, but the numbers so affected were comparatively small; for the bulk of those who had fallen on evil days there was no regular means available for relief.

The problem at last came to a head during the reign of

Queen Elizabeth, and the scheme of Poor Relief instituted during her reign remained the basis of all Poor Law legislation until 1929. The Act of 1601 summarised the experience gained during the previous decades in administering relief. The Act appointed Overseers in each Parish; they were responsible for levying a rate, and, with the Churchwardens, for administering these funds for the benefit of the poor of the Parish. The point to notice is that the responsibility for dealing with the matter was put upon the Parish, and any in need of relief had to apply to the Overseers of the Parish of their birth. Naturally no Parish was anxious to have to deal with the poor from another area as well as its own, so that a system was brought into operation of granting licences to a certain number of beggars, giving them permission to beg alms outside their own Parishes.

Workhouses were set up in the eighteenth century where the aged and destitute could find relief, but by the beginning of the nineteenth century the increase in population and various industrial changes had once more aggravated the problem, and a Royal Commission was set up in the reign of William IV to investigate the whole problem of the Poor Law. The consequent Parliamentary Act of 1834 remained in force for nearly a century. By this act the country was divided up into a number of Unions, each controlled by an elected Board of Guardians who were concerned solely with Poor Relief and nothing else. A Poor Law Commission of three had powers to supervise the Boards of Guardians. The areas administered by the various Unions differed considerably in size and very often they cut across other local government areas and so helped to increase confusion of authorities. The Boards of Guardians had considerable powers. There were two methods of relief which they could employ: *Indoor Relief* meant maintenance in some kind of institution, such as the workhouses, infirmaries, casual wards, cottage homes, etc.; *Outdoor Relief* was maintenance by means of grants of money or supplies of food, but did not necessitate living in any institution. The system worked inequitably according to the sympathies or prejudices of the Guardians, and there was no adequate control from the centre.

At the beginning of this century it was felt that the whole position was unsatisfactory. Readers of Dickens' *Oliver Twist* will have a knowledge of how the workhouse was run in those days, and will understand that no one went there except in sheer despair. To receive Parish relief was regarded as a stigma. The Friendly Societies (see p. 13) saved thousands from "going on the Parish" but the low standard of wages, especially in country districts, meant that the financial resources were too small to do more than give help for short periods.

A Royal Commission was set up and produced a report in 1909 that is a very valuable social document, and was the work of a number of distinguished social economists and public men. No action was taken by Parliament immediately and the first World War postponed the matter still longer. At length, however, the problem was taken up by Parliament and dealt with in the Poor Law Act of 1927 and the Local Government Act of 1929.

Under the new scheme the Boards of Guardians disappeared and in their place Public Assistance Committees were set up by County and County Borough Councils. The work of these Assistance Committees was more efficient than that done by many of the old Boards of Guardians. There was, too, a changing attitude towards those in distress; poverty had been regarded as a crime, and it had been thought that the hardships of workhouse life or of that in "houses of correction" (the Bridewells, named after the original in London after the old Royal Palace which was converted to this purpose) would terrify the poor; in this complete success was achieved, but it left the real problem of poverty untouched. Gradually it came to be recognised that distress was not always, nor even in most cases, due to the personal thriftlessness or perversity, but to circumstances over which the worker had no control, such as loss of employment, the low wages that made substantial savings impossible, old age and sickness. So a series of attacks, as they may be called, were made on these causes of poverty.

The Old Age Pensions Act of 1908 was the first onslaught. For some years the idea had been advocated and discussed; commissions and committees were appointed to carry out investigations and make proposals. The Act of 1908 was very limited in its application; a weekly pension of five shillings was granted to those over seventy with less than £21 a year income. Small as this gain was, it established the principle that the community has a responsibility towards the aged who could not support themselves.

The next line of attack was against the insecurity of employment. Two measures were taken. The first was included with health (see next section) in the National Insurance Act of 1911. Certain industries only were at first included; by a system of contributions from employers, the employed, and the State, any unemployed man could draw benefit for a limited period provided payments were up to date; the Friendly Societies co-operated in working the scheme which was extended in 1920 and again in 1940 to cover more classes of workers. The second measure was the setting up of Labour Exchanges in 1909; the purpose of these was to bring together more quickly the employer who wanted men and the unemployed who wanted work.

These various measures were superseded by the National Insurance Act of 1946. Under this scheme nearly everyone between school-leaving age and pensionable age has to contribute a weekly sum towards insurance. This is done by stamping a card with stamps bought at the Post Office. Employers also contribute to the scheme and a further sum comes from the Exchequer. People who are self-employed, e.g. those who run their own businesses, pay higher contributions than those employed at salaries and wages. The standard rates are as follows:

| | Employee | Employer | State |
|---|---|---|---|
| | *s. d.* | *s. d.* | *s. d.* |
| Men | 4 7 | 3 10 | 2 1 |
| Women | 3 7 | 3 0 | 1 7 |
| Boys (under 18) | 2 8 | 2 3 | 1 2 |
| Girls (under 18) | 2 2 | 1 9 | 11 |

The standard rates of benefit are as follows:

| | | Additional allowance for | | | |
|---|---|---|---|---|---|
| | Insured person | Wife | First child of school age | Dependent husband of insured woman | Relative dependant or person caring for insured's child |
| | *s. d.* | *s. d.* | *s. d.* | *s. d.* | *s. d.* |
| Unemployment | 26 0 | 16 0 | 7 6 | 16 0 | 16 0 |
| Sickness | 26 0 | 16 0 | 7 6 | 16 0 | 16 0 |
| Retirement | 26 0 | 16 0 | 7 6 | Nil | Nil |

The retirement age (the expression now used instead of Old Age) is sixty-five years for men and sixty for women.

There are also benefits for maternity, for widows and guardians, and there is a death grant to cover funeral expenses. This last provision may seem strange, but experience has proved that a vast number of poor people have in the past struggled to pay a few pence weekly into burial schemes; some of these were fraudulent and the contributions often out of all proportion to the benefit received. All this is now simplified and the fear of a "pauper's funeral" removed.

It would be out of place here to give all the details of a scheme that has to take into account, as far as practicable, the diverse circumstances of so many millions of people. There are variations in the amount of benefit; rules as to the number of contributions necessary to qualify for benefit, and so on. The point to note is that here we have a comprehensive scheme, unique in history, for giving a sense of security to the members of the community.

One aid outside this scheme should be mentioned; by the Family Allowances Act of 1945 a payment of five shillings a week is made for every child in a family, except the eldest, up to school-leaving age. This is provided by grant from the Exchequer and costs about sixty million pounds a year.

The third line of attack on poverty—the prevention and cure of sickness—is treated separately in the section that follows.

## ii. *Health*

In the section on Public Health (pp. 43–45) something was said of the importance of environment in promoting good health—housing, efficient sanitation, pure water, and so on. The vast strides made in medical science during the past two centuries have meant a great improvement in the treatment of disease and also in the prevention of disease. To-day we put as much emphasis on creating conditions and habits that will prevent illness as we do on curing specific complaints.

When we read the records of families living in the sixteenth century and even later, we are shocked at the number of children who died in infancy. Parents might have a dozen or even more children, but only one or two would survive infancy. There are no statistics for those past periods, but the improvement within the last hundred years is remarkable. The infantile mortality rate, i.e. the number of infants dying under the age of one year out of every thousand born, at two dates illustrates this improvement.

| | | |
|---|---|---|
| England and Wales, | 1870–2 | 156 per thousand |
| ,, ,, | 1946 | 43 ,, |

Many factors have gone to this decrease in the rate, and also to the all-round improvement in health. Our greater knowledge of food values (a development of this century) has meant a better diet; when we read of some of the meals our ancestors consumed even in Victorian times, it is not surprising that the average age of death was much lower than it is to-day. More widely spread education has meant that knowledge of such matters is now passed on by the newspapers, by broadcasting and by the schools. We still have a long way to go in getting rid of false ideas and superstitions which can be traded upon by some unscrupulous makers of 'patent medicines'.

Another measure of progress would be to compare Mrs Gamp of Dickens' *Martin Chuzzlewit* with the District Nurse of to-day. Mrs Gamp is one of the great comic creations of fiction, but her prototype was a menace to life with her ignorance and dirt. So too there has been a notable increase in the efficiency of hospitals. We think of them as places for the treatment of the sick, but in medieval times they were charitable institutions for the care of the needy and aged as well as of the sick. Most of them were founded by monasteries where some care was always available for the poor. Thus in London, St Bartholomew's Hospital dates back to the twelfth century, and St Thomas's to the thirteenth century; both were founded by the Augustinian Canons. It was only by the strenuous efforts of the citizens of London that they were saved after the spoliation of the monasteries.

The development of the hospitals was due to private charity and generosity; there were nearly a thousand of these voluntary hospitals in 1936, ranging from small cottage hospitals to the great teaching hospitals of London and Edinburgh. Their story fills the brightest pages in the history of philanthropy. The increasing costs of maintenance and the growing demands for their services put a great strain on their resources, and appeals for their support became more and more urgent. At the same time the need increased for more hospitals in many areas poorly served. Voluntary effort, wonderful as the results were, could no longer satisfy the need. So the idea of some kind of national health service came to be discussed.

The first step was taken in the National Insurance Act of 1911; reference has already been made to the unemployment section of the Act (see pp. 57–59). A similar method of collecting contributions was employed; stamps of the value of the combined sum from employer and employed had to be bought and stuck on a card for each person employed. It is difficult for us to realise the storm of opposition raised by this modest scheme—for at first it applied only to those with less than £160 a year. Titled ladies held protest meetings and urged that all should refuse to 'lick stamps'; the employed were incited to protest against the small weekly deduction from their wages. Doctors were warned that their livelihoods would suffer. Actually the result was that many a doctor in a poor district was assured of an income; many a kind-hearted man had refrained from demanding fees. In spite of all this, the Act came into operation, and within a short time was working smoothly to the benefit of millions who lived on small wages.

From time to time this first Act was extended in scope. By the National Health Service Act of 1946, the earlier measures were replaced by a comprehensive scheme affecting the whole community, and hospitals became a State responsibility. The funds are partly derived from the contributions under the National Insurance scheme of the same date, so that the weekly payment covers not only unemployment insurance, retirement pensions, and so on, but also treatment for sickness.

Sixteen types of service are provided. It is not possible to do more here than give the list, but this shows the range of the scheme.

1. General hospital and specialist services.
2. Research; bacteriological service; blood transfusion, etc.
3. Health centres.
4. Care of mothers and young children.
5. Midwifery.
6. Health visiting.
7. Home nursing.
8. Vaccination and immunisation.
9. Ambulance services.
10. Prevention of illness; care and after-care.
11. Domestic help.
12. Mental health services.
13. General medical services.
14. Pharmaceutical services.
15. General dental services.
16. Supplementary ophthalmic services.

Regional Hospital Boards will administer hospital services through Hospital Management Committees. One of the aims of the scheme is to see that medical aid and hospital beds are available in all parts of the country.

The County and County Borough Councils are the local health authorities for certain services; i.e.

Health centres,
Care of mothers and young children,
Midwifery,
Health visiting,
Home nursing,
Vaccination and immunisation,
Ambulance services,
Prevention of illness; care and after-care.

There are a number of other ways of raising the standard of health of the community not coming directly under the

National Health Service. These include the medical inspection of school-children, the provision of milk and, where necessary, of meals. A few figures for 1946 (England and Wales) will indicate the extent of these.

| | |
|---|---|
| Number of children inspected | 4,281,000 |
| Number taking dinners | 2,536,000 |
| Number taking milk | 4,395,000 |

CHAPTER VI

# SPECIAL AUTHORITIES

## i. *London*

It seems absurd to start a description of the administration of London by answering the question "Which London?" There are several different Londons: there is for instance the City of London, the administrative County of London, the ecclesiastical See, and the London of the Metropolitan Police; this last area is sometimes called 'Greater London' with a population of over eight millions. To these could be added the Postal Area and the Telephone Area. No two of these 'Londons' coincide in boundaries. It is therefore necessary to be quite clear as to which London we are talking about. This section will deal first of all with the City of London, and secondly with the administrative County of London.

### (*a*) THE CITY OF LONDON

The actual City area is very small. It covers less than one square mile, and for its size and population it is the wealthiest city in the country. Its population at night is 4420 (day population probably half a million) and its rateable value (see p. 75) is nearly £6,314,672. In 1800 the residential population was about 130,000. It has been said, with a certain amount of truth, that although the City of London is thronged during the day it is practically empty at night except for caretakers and cats! The dreadful air-raids of 1940–1 destroyed 164 acres of buildings out of the total of 460 acres. Many famous churches and buildings were destroyed, including a number of the Halls of the City Companies.

The City holds a unique position in the local government scheme of the country due entirely to its historical development for London has always retained an independence and a character of its own. Many of the institutions of the City, such as the Wardmote and the offices of Aldermen, date back to Saxon times when the City was practically an independent State. William the Conqueror found it necessary to make a treaty with the citizens and he granted them a Charter of Privileges and gave them power to retain the special laws which they had enjoyed under Edward the Confessor. This original Charter is preserved at the Guildhall. William, however, built the Tower of London right up against the City walls, not only as his palace but as an indication that the City could not have all its own way. From that time onwards the City of London has preserved its independence, both of kings and Parliament, and has taken a line of its own with regard to policy. We have not space here to detail the interesting story of the history of the City of London, but it is well worth knowing, for it is full of romance and is also an epitome of the history of our country.

The City is governed by the Corporation, at the head of which is the Lord Mayor, and the affairs of the City are discussed and settled by the Court of Aldermen and the Court of Common Council. This is the only instance of a municipality which has a second Chamber. The Common Councillors are elected from twenty-six Wards into which the City is divided, and the twenty-six Aldermen are chosen for life. The Lord Mayor is elected annually at Michaelmas by the Court of Aldermen from two of their own number nominated by another body known as the Court of Common Hall. This is an interesting survival of the days when the City Companies, or Gilds, were all-powerful. The Court of Common Council carries out all the functions of a Metropolitan Borough Council (see below), and in addition has various other powers peculiar to itself. It can, for instance, remodel its own constitution, and it has its own Police Force of about a thousand men who are familiar figures within the City.

The Corporation is also the sanitary authority for the City and manages the great markets at Smithfield, Billingsgate, Islington, Deptford and Leadenhall. For nearly six centuries these market rights have been an important part of the City's privileges, and it would be difficult to over-estimate the importance of the supervision exercised over the supplies of foodstuffs which come in daily. The Corporation has done much to ensure the purity of the actual supplies that come in, and the hygienic conditions under which they are sold.

The Corporation has its own Police Courts held daily at the Mansion House and the Guildhall, and it also has Civil Courts. One important aspect of the work of the Corporation is the effort it has made for preserving and maintaining open spaces outside the London area. One instance may be given. Epping Forest was acquired at a cost of nearly £250,000 in 1882, when the Corporation fought the various vested interests and so preserved the Forest as a public open space for all time. Similar 'lungs' are controlled by the Corporation in West Ham, at Burnham Beeches, at West Wickham and many other places.

Mention has already been made of the ancient Companies or Gilds. Very few of these now carry out any special work in connection with the trades of their names, but they serve a valuable purpose in their administration of the various Trust Funds which they supervise. They have done particularly useful work in the foundation and maintenance of schools and colleges. The Goldsmiths' Company for instance founded a college in 1891 at New Cross and later on presented this to the University of London. The same Company presented the sum of £5000 towards the cost of the production of the *Oxford Dictionary*. Other Companies have done valuable work outside their own immediate interests.

The City has to face a vast problem in rebuilding its devastated areas. There is a natural desire to make it a far more beautiful city than it has been in the past. An ambitious plan was published in 1944 showing the possibilities, such as giving views of St Paul's Cathedral, and a fine embankment along the river. How far this attractive scheme can be realised must depend on the money available; the buying up of property rights alone would cost many millions.

## (*b*) THE COUNTY OF LONDON

The London County Council was created in 1888, and its duties and powers are practically the same as those of the larger County Boroughs. The area administered stretches from Hammersmith in the west to Woolwich in the east, from Hackney in the north to Wandsworth in the south, covering an area of about 120 square miles. The multifarious duties that it carries out include all the normal ones of a County Council, but with everything on a vastly increased scale.

Within the county there are twenty-eight Metropolitan Borough Councils, constituted and given the same powers and duties as provincial Boroughs, but, as the area they cover is one huge town, many of the normal functions performed by the ordinary Borough Council are in the case of London merged into the work of the County Council. Thus the main sewers are provided by the County Council, but other drainage comes within the work of the Metropolitan Boroughs.

In addition to the L.C.C. and the Metropolitan Boroughs there are other bodies who help to organise the life of the greatest city in the world. The largest of all the 'Londons' is the area administered for police purposes. The *Metropolitan Police* were founded in 1829 and were the first 'Bobbies' or 'Peelers' mentioned previously on p. 49. Readers of Dickens are familiar with the figure of the Bow Street Runner, who was an officer attached to Bow Street Police Office and was a member of what was really the first detective force in the country. The Bow Street Runner became in course of time the detective as we know him in these days as a member of the C.I.D. (Criminal Investigation Department) at New Scotland

Yard, the headquarters of the Metropolitan Police Force. The C.I.D. is primarily concerned with the detection of crime and the capture of criminals within the Metropolitan Police area. They have no power to interfere outside that area unless their expert experience is called in by the police authorities of other counties and boroughs. There is of course close working between all the various police forces, but Scotland Yard cannot step in unless it is requested to do so. The Metropolitan Police are not controlled by the L.C.C. or the boroughs, but by the Secretary of State for Home Affairs. There is a special section known as the Thames Police, recruited from sailors, for the purpose of patrolling the River Thames.

The *Metropolitan Water Board* took over in 1902 the private companies that were responsible for the supply of water to London. The survival of the word 'conduit', in names of streets, is a reminder of those days. The water comes chiefly from the Thames, the River Lea, the New River and various wells and springs. The reservoirs alone cover an area of 1556 acres; the King George's Reservoir in the Lea Valley holds 3,000,000,000 gallons; a daily average of over 332,000,000 gallons is used in Greater London.

The *Port of London Authority* was established in 1909, to administer the tidal portion of the river below Teddington which forms the Port of London, a distance of seventy miles. The duties of the Thames Conservancy Board were then taken over by the authority for that part of the river. *Trinity House* is responsible for the buoying and pilotage of the 'River', though its chief duty is the maintenance of lighthouses round the coast.

The *Thames Conservancy Board* is now chiefly concerned with the improvement of navigation and the prevention of pollution.

## ii. *Scotland*

Local government in Scotland was completely reorganised by the Act of 1929. The general principles have much in common with those which are to be found at work in England and Wales, but generally speaking the local authorities in Scotland are less controlled by the central authority than is customary in England.

The central authority is represented by the Secretary of State for Scotland (see p. 102). The most important authorities for local government are the thirty-three County Councils and the Councils of the twenty-four large Burghs. These authorities have to prepare schemes for the approval of the Secretary of State for the administration of education, public assistance, public health, lunacy and mental deficiency, and, in the case of County Councils, roads and police. They can delegate any of their powers to the Councils of small Burghs (those with a population of less than 20,000) or to District Councils, or to Joint Committees consisting of local representatives and members of the County or Town Council.

There is nothing quite corresponding to the Urban and Rural District Councils of England and Wales. The nearest parallel terms in Scotland are 'burgal' and 'landward': roughly the small Burghs correspond to the Urban Districts, and the District Councils to the Rural Districts.

There are three types of Town Council. First, the *Royal Burghs* incorporated by Royal Charter, such as Ayr and Perth; secondly, the *Parliamentary Burghs*, such as Falkirk and Paisley, and thirdly, the *Police Burghs*. The first two correspond roughly to the English County Boroughs. Four of the Burghs are known as 'Counties of Cities'—Edinburgh, Glasgow, Dundee and Aberdeen. A Burgh Council consists of the *Provost*, who is elected for three years, *Bailies*, who correspond to Aldermen, and *Councillors*, who hold office for three years.

The work is carried on mainly through committees, the chairman of which is called the *Convener*.

The authorities have considerable powers in the matter of raising loans and over the general organisation of finances. A Burgh may hold a certain amount of property, known as the Common Good. This consists of land, markets, etc., and the resulting income considerably eases the burden of local rates. For instance, Kirkcudbright derives an income of £1500 a year from the Common Good and this sum of money is used for the benefit of the community. In the matter of education there is also a difference. The education authorities are either the Town Council of a large Burgh, or the County Council. There are no small education authorities as there are in England, and in Scotland there is far more power to co-opt persons acquainted with the various districts or those directly interested in education.

## iii. *Northern Ireland*

The system of local government in Northern Ireland is practically the same as in England and Wales; there are a few variations, but these are too slight to call for particular mention.

CHAPTER VII

# HOW IT IS ALL PAID FOR

You must have asked yourself before reaching this chapter, "How are all these things paid for?" The amount of money needed is a very large sum; in 1944–5, for instance, the total expenditure of local authorities in England and Wales was £729,103,000.

There are four sources of income:

1. Local loans,
2. Local fees, rents and profits from services, etc.,
3. Local rates, and
4. Government grants.

Before we examine each of these sources, it is well to remind ourselves that the money ultimately comes from us—the members of the community. There is no mysterious treasure chest to be drawn from either by the local Council or by the Government. The people of the country have to pay the expenses of running it. We should therefore ask ourselves occasionally if we are getting value for our money and if there is any avoidable extravagance.

1. *Local loans.* Sometimes a Council has to undertake an expensive piece of work such as a sewage scheme, or, on a smaller scale, public baths. As such things are going to benefit not only us but coming generations, it is felt that the expenditure should be spread over a period of years. So a loan is raised to which we can contribute as an investment; we shall receive interest on the money we invest and can withdraw the whole when we want to do so; but that interest has to be paid and is therefore an annual charge to be included in the account.

2. *Local fees, etc.* This is a miscellaneous collection of receipts from many sources, such as: rents from house property

belonging to the local authority, allotments, markets, transport, cemeteries, perhaps harbour fees, canal charges, etc. Some of these may not always show a profit, but it is usually felt that the value of the service outweighs the possible loss.

3, 4. *Local rates and Government grants.* It is not always practicable to make a clear distinction between local and national expenses. A road, for instance, is for common, not for local, use, and it is only fair that all should share in its maintenance. Some services have to be provided by law whether the local Council wants to have them or not. If, for instance, each local Council was left to decide what schools it would have, some areas would be badly served. So a national standard is set, and grants from national resources are made so that the standard can be maintained.

The Government raises money by taxes (see p. 145). The local authority raises this direct contribution by rates. The amount of the rate each of those liable has to pay is based on the value of the property occupied. There are exceptions to this broad rule; no rate is levied on agricultural property and only a quarter of the normal rate is paid on industrial property; there are also exemptions or partial exemptions on churches and chapels and some other kinds of property. Assessment Committees are appointed to see that valuations are fair.

The rate, made half-yearly, is fixed by dividing up the expenditure that has to be met amongst the rate-payers according to the value of the property they occupy; each pays the rate on each pound of the rateable value. Suppose, for instance, that the local rate is at five shillings in the pound; then a man occupying property of the annual rateable value of £20 would pay 20 × 5 shillings, or £5. The rate is paid by the occupier of the house, not by the owner unless he himself lives in the house. Lodgers do not pay rates, but their landlords, or landladies, take this into consideration when settling the rent of rooms. At first sight it may seem unfair that lodgers do not pay rates directly since they enjoy all the advantages of the district, but they pay indirectly through their rent and they pay taxes like everyone else.

It will help to make all this clear if we examine an actual Demand Note. This one was issued by a Rural District Council for the half-year ending 31 March 1949, and was for a rate of 7*s.* 9*d.* in the pound. The recipient of the Note occupied a house with garden rated at £35, so the half-year's rate came to £13. 11*s.* 3*d.* The following details are printed on the back of the Note.

## GENERAL RATE SERVICES

The following statement shows how the rate in the pound demanded is made up. It sets out the rate in the pound which would be required to meet the net expenses of each of the principal services, after allowing for specific Government Grants towards the expenses of the services marked* but without allocation to particular services of the Government Grants and other moneys receivable under the Local Government Act, 1948.

These Government Grants and other moneys under the Act of 1948, being in aid of local government expenses generally, cannot be allocated to any particular service. They reduce by the amount shown the total rate which would otherwise be demanded.

SERVICES ADMINISTERED BY THE RURAL DISTRICT COUNCIL

| | *s.* *d.* | *s.* *d.* | *s.* *d.* |
|---|---|---|---|
| *Housing | 1·00 | | |
| Public Health | 6·25 | | |
| Sewerage | ·00 | | |
| Water Supply | 1·00 | | |
| House Scavenging | 3·50 | | |
| Other Services and expenses | 1 7·27 | | |
| | | 2 7·02 | |
| *Deduct* | | | |
| The equivalent in terms of a rate in the pound of: | | | |
| Amount receivable by the Rural District Council under Section 9 of the Local Government Act, 1948 | 10·25 | | |
| Amount receivable by the Rural District Council under Part V of the Local Government Act, 1948 | 1·75 | | |
| Other credits of the Rural District Council (not being Government Grants and moneys) | 1·25 | | |
| | | 1 1 25 | |
| | | | 1 5·77 |

## SERVICES ADMINISTERED BY THE COUNTY COUNCIL

### (a) *General County Purposes*

| | s. | d. | s. | d. | s. | d. |
|---|---|---|---|---|---|---|
| *Education | 3 | 1·175 | | | | |
| *Fire Service | | 5·07 | | | | |
| *Highways and Bridges | 2 | 5·09 | | | | |
| Lunacy and Mental Deficiency | | ·845 | | | | |
| *Police | | 8·82 | | | | |
| *Public Assistance<br>*Services under the National Assistance Act, 1948 (Part III) | | 9·97 | | | | |
| *Public Health<br>*Local Health Services under the National Health Service Act, 1946 | 1 | 1·06 | | | | |
| Other Services and Expenses | 1 | 4·345 | | | | |
| Amount payable to county district council under Part I of the Local Government Act, 1948 | 1 | ·145 | | | | |
| | | | 11 | ·52 | | |
| *Deduct* | | | | | | |
| The equivalent in terms of a rate in the pound of: | | | | | | |
| Exchequer Equalisation and Transitional Grant receivable by the County Council under Part I of the Local Government Act, 1948 | 4 | 4·43 | | | | |
| Amount receivable by the County Council under Part V of the Local Government Act, 1948 | | 3·555 | | | | |
| Other credits of the County Council (not being Government Grants and moneys) | | 3·055 | | | | |
| | | | 4 | 11·04 | | |
| | | | | | 6 | 1·48 |

### (b) *Special County Purposes*

| | s. | d. | s. | d. | s. | d. |
|---|---|---|---|---|---|---|
| *Public Health | | 2·095 | | | | |
| *Other Services and Expenses | | 1·795 | | | | |
| | | | | 3·89 | | |
| *Deduct* | | | | | | |
| The equivalent in terms of a rate in the pound of: | | | | | | |
| Other income or credits of the County Council (not being Government Grants and moneys) | | | | 2·14 | | |
| | | | | | | 1·75 |
| GENERAL RATE IN THE POUND | | | | | 7 | 9·00 |

You will notice that the items are under two main headings; first come the expenses incurred by the Rural District Council itself, and secondly those incurred by the County Council to which the Rural District Council has to contribute its share.

Under each of these two main groups comes a list of deductions from the full cost due to grants made by the Government. The items for which such grants are received are marked by an asterisk. Had there been no such grants from central funds the total rate would have been over fourteen shillings in the pound, or nearly double the actual rate demanded.

The average rate throughout England and Wales for 1947–8 in County Borough Councils was 18*s.* 7*d.* in the pound. The great variations are due to the enormous differences in rateable value. For instance property in Westminster is very valuable; high rents are paid not only for business offices but for private dwellings; so a rate of a penny in the pound brings in £37,781. But in another part of London, the Borough of St Pancras, the property is of low value and includes houses in which poorer people live. There a penny rate brings in £8050. So if St Pancras wants to spend £1000 it has to impose a much higher rate than would be needed to bring in the same sum in Westminster. Such inequalities will be found all over the country, and no one has yet found a way of overcoming the difficulty. A partial aid is that the Government can make special grants to local authorities most affected in this way.

CHAPTER VIII

# HOW WE CAN HELP

To qualify as an elector at a local government election you must be of full age (twenty-one), a British subject, and either resident for a minimum period of six months in the area or have a non-resident qualification. Men and women are on an equality. The non-resident qualification applies to members of the forces and to a few others for special reasons. These electors can vote by post or by proxy, and the same method is allowed to the blind and to others physically incapacitated. There are a few disqualifications such as lunacy or imprisonment. The Registration Officer (usually the Town Clerk or someone of his standing) is responsible for preparing the annual Register of Electors; this generally covers both local and parliamentary needs. This Register is to be seen at the Town Hall, at Post Offices and at the Public Library. If anyone believes he has a right to vote, he should make sure his name is on the Register.

Elections are conducted with the greatest safeguards to ensure complete secrecy for each voter; there are severe penalties for any corrupt practices such as intimidation or bribery.

An elector goes to the polling station (usually a school) assigned to him; when he enters he gives the clerk his electoral number which is then crossed off the list. He is given a voting or ballot paper having on it the names of the candidates. He takes this to a screened-off desk where he marks with a cross the name or names for which he wishes to vote. If he makes any other marks, such as signing his name, his paper may be disqualified. After marking the paper, he folds it and puts it in a slit in the sealed ballot box. When the voting period is over the boxes from all the polling stations are taken under guard to the Town Hall, and are there opened in the presence of the candidates or their representatives. The officially appointed tellers then count the votes, and a declaration of the result is made as soon as possible.

If you are an elector one important way in which you can help the community is to vote at all elections. It is sometimes said that we get the Government we deserve; it is just as true to say that we get the Local Councils we deserve. The tendency for some years has been for only a low proportion of the electorate to vote; this is a pity as a lively electorate is the best way of ensuring intelligent local government and administration.

Those who are not yet electors should not put off studying local conditions and problems until their names are put on the Register. There is much to be learned and the greater our knowledge, the greater will be the value of our contribution to local government when the time comes.

Books can help us in our search for knowledge. Some may feel the need for guidance in mental discipline; they would find *Clear Thinking* by R. W. Jepson (Longmans) a useful book.

Here are a few books that will increase your knowledge of local government.

*Local Government in England and Wales*, by W. E. Jackson (Pelican).
*Local Government in Modern England*, by Sir John Maud (Home University Library).

These two short books cover far more ground than is possible in these pages. The second contains a list of more advanced and specialised books for further study. Books of this kind may be out of date in some details even in the latest edition, but the general picture is reliable.

A standard book, going into far greater detail than the above, is

*Local Government of the United Kingdom*, by J. J. Clarke (Pitman).

This should be available in any public library; if it is not in yours, put the title down in the Suggestion Book. It is revised from time to time. There is an abridged version which may be all you need, entitled

*Outlines of Local Government*, by J. J. Clarke (Pitman).

If the historical development of local government interests you, then a good beginning may be made with

*A Century of Municipal Progress*, by various authors (Allen & Unwin).

This covers the period 1835—1935.

Should you wish to go further back in history, then the standard book on local government up to 1835 is the work by Sidney and Beatrice Webb which is published in six volumes by Longmans. These have a forbidding appearance, but you will find them full of interesting information. The titles are:

*The Parish and the County*,
*History of Trade Unionism*,
*The Manor and the Borough*, 2 vols.,
*The Story of the King's Highway*,
*Statutory Authorities for Special Purposes*.

A book of a different type that you may find most helpful if you want to study local history is

*The Parish Chest*, by W. E. Tate (Cambridge University Press).

This opens up all kinds of inviting pathways of research.

It is important to know where to find the facts about any subject. The local newspaper should be a good beginning; it usually contains reports of Council meetings and summaries of reports made to the Council on such subjects as housing, education, and public health. Cuttings should be kept and arranged by subjects. The public library will also provide information; it is usually possible to see there copies of the minutes of Council meetings and of the reports of Committees, and of the County officials. These officials are glad to give information to those who are intelligently interested, and the local Councillors should also be asked for explanations of policy.

## PROBLEMS

An excellent way of sorting out the facts is to try to find answers to definite questions; this can be more effective if done by a group of friends who by discussion and by pooling their knowledge can investigate a problem more thoroughly than a single person can do by himself; even one companion in this work more than doubles the value to be derived from it.

Here are a few typical questions and problems for such discussions and inquiries.

1. Each of the Articles of the Declaration of Human Rights (pp. 7–11) will supply a good subject for a debate. How many of these rights remain to be fully realised in this country?
2. Would local government be more efficient if all the small authorities (e.g. District Councils) were merged into the County? Would anything be gained, and what lost, by dividing the country into large regions instead of continuing to keep the present queer-shaped Counties as the units?
3. Would it be fairer to base rates on income instead of on property?
4. How could the planning of your town or village be improved?
5. Has your local or County Council provided (*a*) public library, (*b*) swimming bath, (*c*) museum and art gallery?
6. Where can children play? Are you satisfied with the provision for them? If not, what would you suggest should be done?
7. Are there any slums in your area? What is being done to get rid of them? What more should be done?
8. How would you answer a grouser who is constantly saying, "The rates must be reduced!"? If you agree with him, suggest how the reduction could be made.
9. What is the function of trade unions to-day? It has been said that they have accomplished their main task; do you agree?
10. Should Co-operative Societies pay the same taxes as other trading concerns?

If you can get together a few enthusiastic people as a team or group, there are some interesting possibilities. For instance, you might compile a local Domesday Book. Each member of the group would investigate one branch of the subject—taking the one that appeals to his own interests. Here is a list of possible divisions of the survey.

1. *Geographical features*—boundaries, soil, rivers, etc.
2. *Historical development*—ancient buildings, charters, etc.
3. *Industries*—old and new, factories, trade unions, etc.
4. *Transport*—roads, railways, canals, etc.
5. *Public Services*—water, light, sanitation, etc.
6. *Education*—schools, evening classes, etc.
7. *Religion*—churches, activities, etc.
8. *Social*—clubs, sports, theatres, cinemas, etc.
9. *Amenities*—baths, parks, libraries, etc.
10. *Law and Order*—police, magistrates, etc.

This list does not exhaust the possibilities and some other grouping may prove more suited to your needs.

Some of the information can be recorded on outline maps; cuttings from newspapers, extracts from reports of Council departments, pictures, as well as notes collected personally by interviews or observation will all form part of the material. Some system of filing the information must be devised; one important rule is that each fact, or convenient group of facts, should be entered on a separate sheet of paper; this makes it easier to shuffle and reshuffle the material according to the immediate need. This is desirable as no arrangement of subjects will produce water-tight compartments; education, for instance, may call for notes about the libraries; and the work of voluntary organisations may be considered under the heading 'Social' or the heading 'Education'.

Such a survey will take a long time, but if the results are preserved then another group may take up unfinished inquiries; so, in time, the local Domesday Book can be compiled. Perhaps the records can be deposited in the public library, or elsewhere, for the use of others who cannot themselves spare the time for such research.

Such a survey is not only a fascinating piece of work for those who do it, but it provides them with a mass of information that will help to make their contribution to the community of real value as their opinions will more likely be intelligently formed and not the sport of passing emotions or popular slogans.

All this may seem rather remote from our day-to-day lives and may make no appeal to you. Are there other ways in which we can help the community? Those who seriously want to do so rarely find it difficult to discover some form of service suited to their abilities and tastes. Helping to organise a dramatic society or a chess club or a cricket club is rendering help to the society in which we live. Then there are organisations for the training of boys and girls and young people in their leisure time; some are run in association with a church or an institution; others are independent but come within the range of the Service of Youth sponsored by the Ministry of Education. Boys' and Girls' Clubs, Scouts and Guides, as well as juvenile sports clubs, all need helpers who are willing to give up some part of their spare time.

We vary considerably in our abilities and tastes; few may want to take an active part in local politics; it is, however, of the utmost importance that men and women of high ideals and with a genuine desire to serve the community should be on our Councils; those who feel drawn in this direction cannot begin too early to study the problems of local government, and by experience in voluntary associations become accustomed to committee work, to the right conduct of meetings, and to expressing their views in a clear and logical manner. We may be tempted at times, perhaps with cause, to say hard things about our local Council; we must remember that the quality of the work of a Council depends on the quality of its members.

# THE NATIONAL COMMUNITY

CHAPTER IX

## THE CONSTITUTION

An eminent American scholar has made the statement that "the English Constitution has made the circuit of the globe and become the common possession of civilised man". This complimentary exaggeration serves to emphasise an aspect of our political organisation which we often overlook. This influence exerted over other countries makes it important for us to understand the nature of the British constitution, and how it has gradually taken shape through the centuries.

It should first be understood that we have no written constitution. That is to say we cannot point to any one statute which describes the constitution in detail. We have no single document such as the written Constitution of the United States of America. It has been pointed out how large a part custom has played in the development of our local government, and the same principle applies to the growth of central government. As Bagehot said:

We have made, or rather stumbled on, a constitution which—though full of every species of incidental defect, though of the worst *workmanship* in all out-of-the-way matters of any constitution in the world—yet has two capital merits: it contains a simple efficient part which, on occasion, and when wanted, *can* work more simply and easily, and better, than any instrument of government that has yet been tried; and it contains likewise historical, complex, august, theatrical parts, which it has inherited from a long past—which *take* the multitude—which guide by an insensible but an omnipotent influence the associations of its subjects. Its essence is strong with the strength of modern simplicity; its exterior is age. Its simple essence may, *mutatis mutandis*, be transplanted to many very various countries, but its august outside—what most men think it is—is narrowly confined to nations with an analogous history and similar political materials.

KINGSHIP AND ASSEMBLY

## i. *Development*

Although the Romans occupied this country for some four centuries they left practically no mark on the political growth of the country. It was during the period between the leaving of the Romans and the coming of the Normans that some of the main principles of our constitution took shape. The various Teutonic and Scandinavian invaders of this country, whom we group together under the name of Anglo-Saxon, brought with them their own tribal customs and methods of government. Their organisation was based on the family and tribe, and the idea of an all-powerful monarch was not to their liking. The leaders of these tribes and families would meet together periodically for deciding matters of dispute and for laying down laws. The important thing to notice is that from the beginning there was the idea of an assembly of Elders and not the idea of one man imposing his will upon everybody. In spite of the changes that have taken place in the course of our history, this principle of the assembly has never been entirely lost. Even when kings controlled various parts of the country, and later when one king ruled all, the practice of the counsel of the Elders being taken was preserved. We may say in brief that the history of our political organisation is the story of the development of these two elements, Kingship and Assembly.

Before the Norman Conquest the Witan (the leading thegns and ecclesiastics) was recognised as an important factor in the government of the country. The principle established in Anglo-Saxon times that the King governs under advice has been a powerful influence in our development. During the Saxon period the order of succession was decided by the Witan, and William the Conqueror himself was careful to gain its approval. There was a feeling that the King should be of royal lineage, but the eldest son as such had no unquestioned right of succession. It was not until James I came from Scotland that the idea of an hereditary title to the throne of England by divine right was put forward, and the insistence of the House of Stuart on that conception was one of the causes of the greatest upheaval this country has known.

The constitution as we know it to-day really begins with the Norman Conquest, when for the first time the idea of centralised rule was carried out. Although William the Conqueror insisted on the power of the throne he was careful to allow local institutions to function as before. The feudal system, which we associate with his name, was not such a rigid affair as history would sometimes have us think. The system implied a chain of authority passing down from the King to the humblest subject, each having his place in the chain and linked up by responsibilities and duties to those below and above him. Perhaps the Normans' most valuable contribution was in the enforcement of justice by sending round itinerant Justices, who represented the King and not the local lord, and so brought a measure of justice to all men (see pp. 148–149).

At that period there were two advisory bodies which were gathered round the King. There was the Great Council, or Magnum Concilium, and the King's Council, or Curia Regis. These were by no means representative bodies in the sense that we would understand the term to-day. They were mainly composed of the King's tenants-in-chief (the leading ecclesiastics and barons) whose opinions were helpful to him. The first of these bodies, the Great Council, was the successor of the Witan, and during William the Conqueror's reign it was called together three times a year. The Saxon Chronicle records that "Thrice a year King William wore his Crown every year he was in England; at Easter he wore it at Winchester; at Pentecost at Westminster; and at Christmas at Gloucester".

The King's Council was a smaller body drawn from the Great Council, and it carried out the government of the country under the King during the intervals when the main body did not meet.

It would be tedious to detail all the steps in the development of our constitution, and those who are interested should read some of the books suggested in Chapter XVIII. All we can do here is to indicate some of the main stages of that development.

The reign of Henry II (1154–89) was notable for the strengthening of the central government and for Henry's insistence on the rule of law. His son John (1199–1216), not having his father's political insight, attempted to put the clock back and thus involved himself in a dispute with the barons and ecclesiastics. The outcome of that dispute was the signing of Magna Carta on 15 June 1215. This has always rightly been regarded as a landmark in our history. There are one or two interesting points about the Charter which need emphasising. It was not the result of a popular demand but was the work of the nobles and leading bishops. Nor did it lay down any new principles; it was a restatement of old customs and laws. Its greatest value was its insistence on the fact that the Law was above the King. In reading through the Charter it will be noticed how often ancient liberties and ancient customs are referred to, and we shall find that this method of making progress by building on the custom of the past has been followed all through our history. At this time also the power of the purse began to be felt. When the King needed money he was forced to appeal for help to the Council, and many a hard bargain was made in exchange for granting supplies. It is worth noting that in 1213 John summoned to his aid representatives of the shires; we do not know if this assembly ever met, but the idea was to prove fruitful.

Under Henry III (1216–72) there was again a dispute between the King and his chief councillors, and in 1265 Simon de Montfort, the leader of the barons, called together a Parliament that included for the first time representatives from some of the boroughs. Edward I's Parliament of 1295 has been referred to as the Model Parliament, because a step further was made in securing a more representative assembly. Three groups were represented: the Nobles, the Church, and the Commons. As most of the clergy, however, were also feudal lords they inevitably united with the Nobles, and so we get two groups, the Lords Spiritual and Temporal, and the Commons, and not three distinct Estates, as in pre-Revolution France, of Nobles, Clergy, and Commons.

These early Parliaments were called at very irregular intervals and membership of them was by no means regarded as a thing to be sought, as attendance involved the great expense of travelling and all the dangers of the road.

The troublesome times of the Hundred Years' War and the Wars of the Roses had little effect on constitutional development or indeed on the ordinary people of the country. The coming of the Tudors in 1485 marks the next important stage in our history. Henry VII was determined to deliver the country and himself from the control of the baronial party. He therefore tended to put more reliance on the merchant class, and his successors adopted the same policy. The Privy Council, which was derived from the Great Council, became the most important body for administration, but the Tudors were always careful to seek for the support of the Commons, and during their reigns the prestige and influence of the Commons increased considerably. During the last years of Elizabeth's long reign there were indeed already signs that that power would be extended.

James I's insistence on absolute rule, followed by the similar policy of Charles I, brought the question of Parliamentary control to a head. James I had neither the tact nor the wisdom of Elizabeth and he was foolish enough to put into words and action what she may indeed have thought, but was wise enough not to carry into practical politics. In one speech to Parliament James said "Monarchy is the supremest thing upon earth... as to dispute what God may do is blasphemy, so is it sedition in subjects to dispute what a King may do in the height of his power". He had, however, more wisdom than his son; they were going against the deepest principles of the English people, especially that principle of kingship controlled by advisers that dates back to the time of the Anglo-Saxons. The Civil War meant the end of absolute rule in England, though this involved a brief experience of the rule of force. The Restoration Settlement under Charles II was in the nature of a compromise, the principle being accepted that sovereignty resides in the King *and* his Parliament. Charles II was too astute to try to upset that settlement, but his brother James II, a Stuart of the Stuarts, once more attempted to override Parliament. The country then called in William of Orange and his wife Mary, the daughter of James II, as King and Queen, and in 1689 the Bill of Rights restated once more the principles of the constitution, and that document is the nearest approach we have to a statutory declaration of the constitution of this country.

Since 1688 development in various directions has been gradual. The supremacy of Parliament has become a matter of fact, and the personal rule of the King has gradually declined in spite of attempts by George III to emphasise the royal power. The Commons have taken the leading part in Parliament and have gradually become more representative and democratic. Since the settlement of 1689 two important developments have taken place. The first is the growth of the Cabinet System, that is to say an inner circle of leaders who decide on the main lines of policy, and the second, the rise of political parties and of the party system. Neither of these developments has any statutory authority, but by custom they have become part of the regular political organisation, so much so that we not only speak of His Majesty's Government, but of His Majesty's Loyal Opposition.

It is almost impossible to describe our constitution by a single term, since it connotes the whole body of rules, customs, practices and laws by which the government is carried on. Sometimes it has been called a Limited Monarchy and sometimes a Democratic Monarchy. It has even been suggested that the term 'Crowned Republic' would be suitable, but such words can do little more, at the best, than indicate a very rough idea of the nature of the constitution. It has already been pointed out that our present system of government has developed slowly without any preconceived paper scheme. One result of this is that when we examine the nature of the constitution we find much that is illogical and anomalous. In this it reflects the character of the English people. As a nation we are not fond of clear-cut systems; we prefer to express ourselves in action, and to find a means of action through compromise rather than make no movement at all.

There are, however, a number of elements that we can distinguish in the make-up of the constitution, and a brief consideration of these will help to clarify our ideas. First of all there are a number of documents and statutes which define certain functions, such as Magna Carta, 1215, the Bill of Rights, 1689, the Act of Settlement, 1701, the Acts of Union of 1707 and 1800, and the Reform Acts from 1832 onwards. Secondly there are a number of important judicial decisions made in the Courts of Law, such as Bushell's Case in 1670, which established the independence of juries. Thirdly there are a number of rules of Common Law, (see p. 152) that is, the law as laid down by judges, based on the customs and practices of the people. Most of the above concern matters which are enforceable by law, but there is a fourth element known as 'the Conventions' which consist of various understandings and practices not set out in any statute. Of these we may instance the fact that the Prime Minister is by custom the leader of the largest party.

The recital of these elements in the constitution stresses the impossibility of reducing it to a formula, for not only is the constitution undefined by Act of Parliament, it has never been regarded as sacrosanct. Whereas in the United States of America, or France, any attempt to change the constitution would be regarded as almost a political crime, we in this country adapt the constitution to meet new conditions. Thus it has been said: "Our Parliament can make laws protecting wild birds or shellfish, and with the same procedure can break the connections of Church and State, or give political power to 2,000,000 citizens and redistribute it among new constituencies". All this has appeared to some foreigners as so extraordinary that some have gone so far as to say that there is no such thing as a British constitution at all!

## ii. *The Crown*

In considering the details of how the government of the country works it is best to begin with the King and the Crown, and here at once we are faced with one of those subtle distinctions that are so confusing in theory but so simple in practice. The King is a person; the Crown is an idea. We speak of His Majesty's Navy or H.M. Stationery Office, but this does not mean that they are the personal property of the King as a person; they belong to the Crown. Perhaps the distinction can be made clear by saying that the Crown is the supreme authority in the country and consists of a working combination of Sovereign, Ministers and Parliament. Practically all the powers of the King as a person have been transferred to the Crown as the executive authority. The Crown enforces all laws; it directs administration; it expends money voted by Parliament; it appoints judges, and also officers to the Army, Navy and Air Forces. It supervises local government and controls foreign relations with other Powers; it bestows peerages, and summons Parliament; it gives or withholds assent to Bills, though the veto has not been used since 1707, and finally the Crown is the effective head of the Churches of

England and of Scotland. These powers are exercised, not by the King as a person, but through the Privy Council, the Cabinet and the Ministers, so that it is quite true to say "The King can do no wrong", since whatever he does is done with the authority of the Ministers of the Crown.

It has already been pointed out that kingship in this country is on a conditional basis. This fact has been emphasised very effectively by the execution of Charles I (1649) and by the final expulsion of the Stuarts in 1688. The present line of Kings goes back to the Act of Settlement of 1701, when it was provided that should there be no heirs to the throne of William III or of Anne, the throne should "be, remain, and continue to the most excellent Princess Sophia, and the heirs of her body, being Protestants". Sophia was a granddaughter of James I and the mother of the Hanoverian Prince who ascended the throne in 1714 as George I. King George V's title read "George V, by the Grace of God, of Great Britain, Ireland, and the British Dominions beyond the Seas, King, Defender of the Faith, Emperor of India". In this title much history is summarised. "Defender of the Faith" takes us back to the time of Henry VIII before the break with Rome. The phrase "British Dominions beyond the Seas" was first used in the Proclamation of 1901, and the title of "Emperor of India" was assumed by a Royal Proclamation in 1876. It was deleted when the Dominions of India and Pakistan achieved self-government in 1947.

On his accession the King is now required to declare "that he is a faithful Protestant, and that he will, according to the true intent of the enactments which secure the Protestant succession to the throne of the Realm, uphold and maintain the said enactments to the best of his powers according to law".

The finances of the King, apart from his private possessions, are provided by the Civil List. This amounts annually to £410,000, with additional grants for members of the Royal Family other than the King and Queen.

Although the personal executive power of the King has been almost reduced to nothing he still has a large measure of influence both in the Government and in his Dominions. It is true that he may not perform public acts except on the advice of the Ministers, for which they are responsible to Parliament, but he has to exercise a number of functions independently of Parliament. It is for instance by his personal choice that a member of Parliament is invited to form a Ministry, and his assent is necessary for a dissolution of Parliament. It is true that various customs indicate the usual line of action, but the decision is ultimately his. The outgoing Prime Minister submits his advice, but circumstances may be complicated. When the Labour Government resigned in 1931 the position was unique. A General Election was not desired at such a critical time. It was probably the personal decision of George V that led to the outgoing Prime Minister, Mr Ramsay MacDonald, becoming Prime Minister of a coalition.

The King's most valuable function is as general adviser. Ministries come and Ministries go; the constant factor is the King. After some years of experience the King gains a knowledge of affairs and of personalities that enables him to give valued advice. Many Prime Ministers have borne testimony to the help they received from Queen Victoria, from Edward VII or from George V. It is rare now for the King to make a direct move in politics, but there have been occasions during this century when such actions have been taken and have resulted in definite progress. King George V, for instance, in 1914, when Irish affairs were critical and a deadlock had arisen, called together a conference of the leaders of all parties at Buckingham Palace and appealed to them to find a means out of the difficult situation. His action was criticised in some quarters, but it undoubtedly eased the position.

Not the least of the functions of our King is the dignity and pageantry he brings into State affairs: it is a mistake to decry the importance of ceremony. Whatever we may say, we all enjoy it and it helps to strengthen those sentiments of loyalty and pride that are part of our patriotism.

Since the Imperial Conference of 1926, when the equality of the self-governing Dominions was recognised, the King as a person has become the great bond which unites the British Commonwealth of Nations. He has been called "The Golden Link of Empire", and it would be difficult to emphasise too much the importance of the King as the representative of unity.

CHAPTER X

# THE CABINET AND THE MINISTRIES

When we grumble about 'The Government' and say 'IT' should do this or that, of whom are we thinking? Often we use the word 'Government' rather loosely, but if we had to be more precise we should probably say 'the Prime Minister and the Cabinet'. The fact that neither the Prime Minister nor the Cabinet had, until recently, any legal existence, is a good illustration of how our constitution can develop according to need, and is not a rigid system. The first Act of Parliament to mention the Prime Minister was the Chequers Estate Act of 1917, and the Ministers of the Crown Act of 1937 referred to Ministers of Cabinet rank; it also provided a salary for the Leader of His Majesty's Opposition, thus giving him a legal standing.

Even to-day, Ministers are not called to a 'Cabinet Meeting' although that is the expression used in the newspapers and broadcast; they are summoned to a meeting of 'His Majesty's Servants'. This phrase takes us back to the days when the members of the King's household looked after the accounts and transacted all business; it was difficult in the Middle Ages to separate the King's business from the State's business. Another relic of those days survives in the appointments to His Majesty's Household that are made by the Prime Minister —such as the Captain of the King's Bodyguard of the Yeomen of the Guard.

The Cabinet under the Prime Minister is responsible for general policy and is itself responsible to Parliament; this, in effect, means to the House of Commons, which, in its turn, is responsible to the whole community.

## i. *Development*

The origin of the Cabinet is to be found in the history of the Privy Council. In the Middle Ages, the King's Council, or Privy (i.e. private) Council, was an advisory body consulted by the King; the members were those concerned with administration, such as the Treasurer and the Chancellor, with such of the prelates and lords as the King chose to have about him. Under the Tudors, the Privy Council became a more regular body with considerable duties; committees of the Council were appointed for special purposes, such as the 'Council in the Star Chamber'. At the same time, the House of Commons was given a greater share in affairs, and this ultimately meant a decline in the position of the Privy Council. The increased responsibility of the Commons inevitably resulted in a closer scrutiny by the members of the work of other parts of the government. The clash between King and Parliament that led to civil war may be regarded as a dispute on this question of responsibility. James I and Charles I wished this to remain in their power; Parliament felt that it should not be left to the King to decide whose advice he should take. The problem became more acute because the King's revenues were no longer equal to the expenses of government; hence the need for more money brought up the question of taxation. Parliament's attitude to this (as shown in the case of John Hampden and Ship Money) was that since the money had to come from the people, Parliament had the right to say how much should be raised, how it should be raised and how it should be spent. "He who pays the piper, should call the tune." In the next century the American colonists, many of whose ancestors had left England during the dispute between King and Parliament, made the same claim. So gradually the House of Commons was to win the control of finance and, ultimately, of policy.

The Privy Council did not suddenly cease to have authority.

Charles II preferred to consult a few members of the Council rather than the whole body; this saved time by avoiding awkward discussions. He naturally selected those who would be likely to support his views. The initial letters of the names of one such group of personal advisers, Clifford, Arlington, Buckingham, Ashley and Lauderdale, happened to form the word 'Cabal'—a term already in use for a secret committee or 'cabinet council'; the word 'cabinet' implied that the meeting was held in a small room or cabinet; another name used was 'Junto'; these names were not intended to be complimentary as such meetings of a few favoured councillors were regarded with suspicion.

When William and Mary came to the throne an attempt was made to revive the full meetings of the Privy Council to discuss policy with the King; but it was soon found that decisions were delayed and business hindered by lengthy argument. So inevitably a few leading Councillors were called together by the King as a 'cabinet council': in this way preliminary decisions could be taken before business came up at the Privy Council or in Parliament.

It was not long before the important question was asked—"How was this small group of advisers to be chosen?" It was felt that the King should not select them according to his personal inclinations as this might mean unending contention between the cabinet council and Parliament. The answer was worked out gradually during the eighteenth century. Four important principles were eventually established:

(i) the Cabinet must have the support of the majority of the members of the House of Commons,
(ii) the members of the Cabinet must be either members of the House of Lords, or of the House of Commons,
(iii) the King must accept the advice of the Cabinet, and
(iv) the Cabinet is collectively responsible for the advice it gives.

This process might have taken longer than it did but for one of those chance situations arising that influence the course of history. George I was more interested in Hanover than in England and he could not speak English; he was therefore content to leave affairs to the Whig party, who could be relied on to support the Hanoverians; the Tories were tainted with Jacobitism. In Sir Robert Walpole the King found an ideal adviser who could talk to him in bad Latin and not bother him too much. George II wisely followed his father's example, so from 1721 to 1742 Walpole dominated the political scene; the strict discipline he exercised over his fellow ministers gave greater cohesion to the Cabinet and he laid the foundations of the present position the Cabinet has in the constitution. His enemies dubbed him 'Prime Minister' in derision; once more a term of opprobrium was to become one of respect. In 1735 Walpole went to live at No. 10 Downing Street, and that house has since then remained the official residence of the Prime Minister, and one of its rooms became the Cabinet Room.

The members of the Cabinet and other Ministers of the Crown are members of the Privy Council and use the prefix 'Right Honourable'; Gladstone indeed called the Cabinet 'the operative part of the Privy Council'. The Council consists of past and present Ministers, and other eminent men including statesmen of the Dominions. It no longer has any executive function, but a few of the members are called together from time to time to carry out some formal duties. Its former high position has been lost, but it remains in the background and could, in an emergency, be called into consultation.

## ii. *The Ministers*

Let us now consider the composition of the Ministry as it was at the beginning of 1949.

### MEMBERS OF THE CABINET

Prime Minister and First Lord of the Treasury.
Lord President of the Council and Leader of the House of Commons.
Secretary of State for Foreign Affairs.
Chancellor of the Exchequer.
Minister of Defence.
Chancellor of the Duchy of Lancaster.
Lord Privy Seal and Paymaster-General and Leader of the House of Lords.
Lord Chancellor.
Secretary of State for the Home Department.
Secretary of State for the Colonies.
Secretary of State for Commonwealth Relations.
Secretary of State for Scotland.
Minister of Labour and National Service.
Minister of Health.
Minister of Agriculture and Fisheries.
Minister of Education.
President of the Board of Trade.

### MINISTERS NOT IN THE CABINET

First Lord of the Admiralty.
Secretary of State for War.
Secretary of State for Air.
Minister of Transport.
Minister of Food.
Minister of Town and Country Planning.
Minister of National Insurance.
Minister of Supply.
Minister of Fuel and Power.
Minister of Civil Aviation.
Postmaster-General.
Minister of Works.
Minister of State for Colonial Affairs.
Minister of State.
Minister of Pensions.

It will be instructive to compare the above list with the membership of Gladstone's Cabinet in 1868.

First Lord of the Treasury.
Lord Chancellor.
Lord President of the Council.
Lord Privy Seal.
Chancellor of the Exchequer.
Secretary of State for the Home Department.
Secretary of State for Foreign Affairs.
Secretary of State for the Colonies.
Secretary of State for War.
First Lord of the Admiralty.
Secretary of State for India.
President of the Board of Trade.
Chief Secretary for Ireland.
Postmaster-General.
President of the Poor Law Board.

A careful comparison of these two lists brings out a number of important historical facts. Only nine of the Cabinet offices of 1949 are to be found in Gladstone's list; two of his have disappeared—Secretary of State for India and Chief Secretary for Ireland; those two alone represent much history. Gladstone's 'President of the Poor Law Board' became 'President of the Local Government Board' in 1871, and this was again changed in 1919 to 'Minister of Health'. Here we see a widening of the field of activity and a greater appreciation of the positive aspect of government.

Gladstone's 'Secretary of State for the Colonies' was responsible for all the territories we now call Dominions as well as those that are still Colonies. In 1925 there was a separation of the duties between the Secretary for the Colonies and the Secretary for Dominion Affairs. The last change came in 1947 when the second of these Ministers became Secretary for Commonwealth Relations. Here again the alterations indicate changing functions to meet fresh needs, or developments in our attitudes towards problems. Another example is found in the changed positions of the

Secretary for War and of the First Lord of the Admiralty. These Ministers are not in the 1949 Cabinet, nor is the Secretary for Air (a position undreamt of in 1868). Their Cabinet position is taken by the Minister of Defence, a Ministry created in 1947 to co-ordinate the policy of all Service Ministries.

The names that are not found in the Gladstone Cabinet are self-explanatory and call for no special description. There is, however, one point to notice. The present long list of Ministers shows how greatly the function of government has expanded since 1868; we now expect the Government to deal with many communal needs—food, fuel, transport, aviation, and town and country planning. To a Victorian statesman such expectations would have seemed fantastic. One result, as we shall see, has been a vast increase in the work to be done by Parliament; we are not here concerned to discuss how far this is desirable or not, but it is a fact that should be kept in mind.

The names of the holders of the offices in these two lists have not been given; but it is interesting to note that in the Gladstone Cabinet there were seven peers, and in the 1949 Cabinet only two. This again indicates a change of attitude. The House of Commons likes to have the holder of any important Ministry amongst its own members. By the Ministers of the Crown Act of 1937, it is required that at least three Ministers must be in the House of Lords. The Lord Chancellor is, of course, always one of these. In 1949 there were also three peers amongst the Ministers not in the Cabinet.

It will be noticed that the 1949 list is divided into two groups—members of the Cabinet and Ministers not in the Cabinet. The Ministers of the Crown Act of 1937 fixed the salary of a Minister of Cabinet rank (whether actually in the Cabinet or not) at £5000 a year. The Prime Minister and the Lord Chancellor each receive £10,000, the former having a salary as First Lord of the Treasury and not as Prime Minister! It will be noticed that in the second group there is a Minister entitled 'Minister of State' without any further description. From time to time there is need for the services of someone having the status and prestige of a Minister but without departmental duties; in other countries such a position is sometimes called 'Minister without Portfolio'. The instance in the 1949 list is of a Minister mainly concerned with duties in connection with the United Nations (see p. 209).

The Prime Minister decides who shall be in the Cabinet. Naturally he consults prominent members amongst his supporters but the decision lies with him. Too large a Cabinet means a slowing-up of decisions. The normal number for some years has been about fifteen; in the eighteenth century, six or seven was customary. Even in the present-day Cabinet there is an unofficial inner group of three or four leading Ministers with whom the Prime Minister consults privately. Ministers not in the Cabinet are called into a Cabinet meeting when matters affecting their departments are under discussion.

Some ancient offices no longer carry onerous duties, but they are retained because they make provision for two or three Ministers who are not constantly occupied with the work of an active department of State. This enables them to survey general policy in a more detached manner than other Ministers can do; a Minister in charge of a department is naturally inclined to view matters from that department's needs; he is rightly jealous of its success and progress.

The Prime Minister himself holds office as First Lord of the Treasury; this entails little administrative work and so leaves him free to devote his time to main questions of policy. Other examples in the 1949 list are Lord President of the Council, the Chancellor of the Duchy of Lancaster, and the Lord Privy Seal, all offices that take us far back into our history.

The Lord President of the Council is, under the King, the chief member of the Privy Council and he is usually present at its meetings. There is little for him to do apart from formal business. In 1949 this position was linked with that of Leader of the House of Commons. This entails being in the House (though not always in the Chamber itself) during debates; the Leader is responsible for working out with the Ministers and with the Leader of the Opposition the programme of legislation and debate. A more difficult task is that of sensing the 'feeling of the House' and so promoting smooth working. In this way he relieves the Prime Minister of much irksome detail.

The Chancellor of the Duchy of Lancaster has some administrative duties in connection with the estates attached to the Crown since Henry IV came to the throne; he had been Duke of Lancaster. These duties are not heavy.

The King's Privy Seal was used from the time of King John on documents of secondary importance; in the fourteenth century a Keeper of the Privy Seal was appointed to safeguard its use; he was known as Lord Privy Seal from the sixteenth century. The office is now of little practical significance, but the holder of this historic position ranks high in the order of precedence. In 1949 this position was combined with two others. The Paymaster-General is the agent for making payments on behalf of the Government; as no questions of policy are involved, the duties are largely of a routine character. The position of Leader of the House of Lords entails far more work and responsibility than the two other appointments linked together in 1949. He leads the Government supporters in the Lords, and, in consultation, arranges the business; constant attendance is necessary.

The reference above to the Privy Seal suggests a note on the Great Seal and its keeper, the Lord Chancellor. The Great Seal is used on documents of the highest importance issued in the name of the King. When a new King, or Queen, ascends the throne, the old seal is broken and a new one made. On appointment the Lord Chancellor receives the seal, which is carried on important occasions in an ornate bag. When he resigns, he hands the seal back to the King. The Chancellor's duties are varied and considerable. He is head of the judiciary and is concerned with the appointment of judges and magistrates; much patronage, both ecclesiastical and legal, is in his hands; he presides over sittings of the House of Lords, and while doing so, sits upon the Woolsack, a square red ottoman, the original of which is said to have been a reminder in the days of Edward III of the importance of England's wool trade.

There is no difference between the position of a Secretary of State and that of a Minister except historically. Before Tudor times a Secretary in the King's Household was not a person of great importance, but from the later years of Henry VIII the position gained in influence. When Elizabeth came to the throne she appointed Sir William Cecil (Burghley) as her Secretary of State. From the Restoration there were two Secretaries of State. One of these was for the North and the other for the South; the former was concerned with foreign affairs. As the work of government became more intricate, it became necessary to divide the duties amongst several Secretaries or Ministers. In 1782 the northern department became the Foreign Office, and the southern became the Home Office. A Secretary of State for War was added in 1794 and for half a century he was also responsible for the Colonies, for whom a separate Secretary was appointed in 1856.

On the union with Scotland in 1707 a Secretary for Scotland was appointed; this office lapsed after the 1745 Jacobite Rebellion but was re-established in 1885. The Secretary for Scotland has under him departments for agriculture, education, health, and for Scottish home affairs. This has meant considerable devolution of administration, but not going as far as the Scottish Nationalists would like. There have been agitations from time to time for a similar Secretary for Wales, but this desire is partly met by special administrative arrangements for agriculture, education, health and some other matters.

The Secretary of State for Home Affairs (Home Secretary) is responsible for the maintenance of the King's Peace through the administration of justice, the organisation of the police and the supervision of prisons and other institutions such as Approved Schools (see p. 162). He advises on the exercise of the King's prerogative of mercy. The Home Office is also concerned with public safety (explosives, firearms, etc.), and controls the entry of aliens and the grant of nationalisation. It regulates the holding and conduct of Parliamentary and local elections.

Up to the time of the first World War, the Secretary of State for Foreign Affairs (Foreign Secretary) had more independence of action than any other Minister; this was a survival of the days when foreign policy was more the personal concern of the Sovereign than of Parliament. The tradition had become established that Parliament did not discuss the day-to-day development of foreign policy and need not be fully informed of any negotiations. So, when war broke out in 1914, even some members of the Cabinet were ignorant of our commitments. There was consequently a strong demand for 'open diplomacy' as opposed to 'secret diplomacy'. We are now accustomed to full discussions of these matters and to the journeyings of the Foreign Minister, or of a deputy, to conferences and meetings abroad. It may be that 'open diplomacy' has gone too far, for it has resulted in a certain tendency to 'play to the gallery' in conference speeches; differences are more likely to be solved by calm discussion than by flights of oratory. The important thing is that the nation should be kept informed of progress at each stage of negotiations.

The Foreign Secretary is constantly in touch with the resident ambassadors of foreign countries and with British ambassadors abroad. There are grades of dignity and authority amongst diplomatic representatives. The Ambassador is the direct representative of the Sovereign or President and has full authority to discuss questions with the Foreign Minister of the country to which he is accredited. Next comes the Envoy or Minister Plenipotentiary, that is, with considerable powers. A Chargé d'Affaires may be appointed to act during the absence of an Ambassador or Minister. Sometimes the word 'Extraordinary' is added; this and 'Plenipotentiary' are more matters of dignity than of distinction of authority. All matters of policy are decided not by the Ambassador but by his Government, but the degree of discretion allowed him indicates his standing. The importance of a country may determine the status of the diplomatic representative. Thus in the United States of America we have an 'Ambassador Extraordinary and Plenipotentiary'—a description that would be difficult to exceed in importance; but in Iceland our representative is the 'British Envoy and Minister Plenipotentiary'.

The consular service is not concerned with policy. British Consuls are to be found in all important cities abroad; they look after the legal rights of British subjects, and give advice and, when desirable, assistance to them; part of the service is to study the commercial and trade conditions of the country.

Each Minister has either an Under-Secretary of State or a Parliamentary Secretary as his principal assistant; he is a member of the House of Commons or of the House of Lords. There is also a Parliamentary Private Secretary (unpaid) who is a member of the Commons. This last appointment is generally regarded as a first step to higher office.

The permanent staffing of a Ministry will be described when we consider the Civil Service in Chapter XV.

CHAPTER XI

# PARLIAMENT

"On the left bank of the Thames, midway between Chelsea Bridge and the Tower, stands the largest and most impressive Gothic structure in the world, the Palace of Westminster; and within its massive walls sits, appropriately enough, the oldest, largest, most powerful, and most interesting of modern legislatures. Not only is the British Parliament the principal instrumentality of popular government in one of the most democratic of states; it is, in a very real sense, the 'mother of Parliaments', whose progeny has spread into every civilised quarter of the globe."

This statement has been made by a leading American authority on political science, and our business in this chapter is to understand what is meant by this British Parliament and how it is constituted.

## i. *The House of Lords*

An Act of Parliament opens with the words:

"Be it enacted by the King's most Excellent Majesty, by and with the advice and consent of the Lords Spiritual and Temporal, and Commons in this present Parliament assembled, and by the authority of the same, etc." Let us first consider 'the Lords Spiritual and Temporal'.

The members of the House of Lords may be grouped under five headings:

1. *The Princes of the Royal Blood.* It is very rare indeed for any of these to take an active part in the proceedings of the House of Lords.

2. *Hereditary Peers.* A peerage is passed on by the principle of primogeniture. The heir must accept, he cannot surrender

or transfer his peerage. All the children of a peer are commoners, even though they bear courtesy titles. This is apt to be a little confusing when we hear that Lord So-and-So is a member of the House of Commons, but the title 'Lord' in his case is a courtesy, and should he succeed to the peerage of his father, he would have to vacate his seat in the House of Commons.

3. *Representative Peers.* Since the union of 1707 no new Scottish peers have been created, and consequently the number in existence has dwindled to thirty-two. These elect sixteen of their number to represent them in the House of Lords. Many Scottish peers also hold peerages of the United Kingdom and therefore have seats in the House of Lords by right.

Until the setting up of the Irish Free State in 1920 there were twenty-eight representative Irish peers chosen for life. Since that date no new ones have been elected and in 1949 there were only eight surviving. Irish peers not elected as representatives were allowed to be members of the House of Commons. Lord Palmerston in the last century and the Earl of Winterton in this century are examples of Irish peers in the Commons.

4. *Lords of Appeal.* It is essential that the House of Lords should always contain a number of eminent judges and lawyers as it is the final Court of Appeal. There are seven Law Lords, who are appointed for life.

5. *Lords Spiritual.* These are the representatives of the Church of England, who may be regarded as the constitutional descendants of the Abbots and other ecclesiastics who were summoned to the earliest Parliaments. Not all bishops are members of the House of Lords. Permanent members are the two Archbishops and the Bishops of London, Durham and Winchester. Twenty-one other bishops have seats according to seniority.

There are at present about 850 members of the House of Lords. Their number is added to from time to time by new creations, when peerages are conferred on prominent men. At one time, even within memory, these creations were sometimes due to the use of political and other influence and not due to worth. Within recent years, however, there has been a change in public feeling on the matter, with the consequence that it is felt necessary to justify a new creation. These honours are conferred by the King on the advice of the Prime Minister, and with the approval of the Political Honours Scrutiny Committee.

The whole question of whether a second Chamber is necessary, and if so, what its constitution should be, has been discussed at great length during this century, and various schemes for reform have been suggested. The Bryce Conference on the Reform of the Second Chamber (1917–18) gave the following as the important functions that the House of Lords should fulfil:

1. The examination and revision of Bills brought from the Commons, where possibly owing to pressure of business they have not been fully discussed.

2. The initiation of non-controversial Bills.

3. The interposition of so much delay in the passing of a Bill as to enable the opinion of the nation to find adequate expression.

4. Full and free discussion of important questions of principle and of foreign policy.

The objections to the House of Lords as at present constituted may be stated briefly. The hereditary element is the largest, and however eminent the original holder of a title may have been there is no guarantee that his descendants will inherit his ability. It has been urged with some justice that the Lords on the whole represent only a small part of the national interests and that they have always been mainly conservative in outlook. This has meant a good deal of friction with the Commons when the Government has been Whig, or Liberal, or Labour. There have been occasions when in order to get legislation passed that was urgently demanded by the country as a whole, the Sovereign has undertaken to create a sufficient number of peers to secure a majority in favour of the proposals. In 1712 Queen Anne created twelve peers in order to secure the passing of the Treaty of Utrecht. In 1832, when it looked as though the Reform Bill would be rejected by the peers, the King let it be known that he was prepared to create a sufficient number of new peers to ensure that the Bill would become law. The threat, however, was sufficient and the House of Lords passed the Reform Bill. A similar position arose in 1911. From 1905 a Liberal Ministry with a large majority in the House of Commons passed a number of measures of importance which were rejected one after the other by the House of Lords. A climax was reached in 1909 when the Lords threw out the Finance Bill, or Budget as it is popularly known. It has always been a tradition that finance is the concern of the Commons alone and this interference by the Lords was regarded as unconstitutional. The Government appealed to the country at a General Election and were again returned to power. They then brought in the Parliament Act of 1911 which included the following provisions: first, that any Money Bill, certified as such by the Speaker, which is not passed by the House of Lords without amendment within one month of its being sent up to that House shall become an Act of Parliament on receiving the Royal Assent; and secondly, that any other Bill which has been passed by the House of Commons in three successive sessions shall become an Act of Parliament on receiving the Royal Assent, provided that a period of two years elapses between the second reading in the first of these sessions and the passing of the Bill in the third of the sessions. The Bill also provided that no Parliament could exist for longer than five years. A further appeal was made to the country and once more the Government received a majority, and on the King allowing it to be known that he was prepared to create the necessary number of new peers, the Parliament Act was accepted by the House of Lords. Since that time the question of reform has been very carefully considered and various proposals have been made, and there is no doubt that sooner or later the matter will have to be reopened and settled. In 1948 the Commons passed a Bill reducing the delaying period from two years to one; under the Parliament Act this became law in 1950.

## ii. *The House of Commons*

Whereas the House of Lords is mainly hereditary, the House of Commons is entirely elective. Membership is open to British subjects of either sex above the age of twenty-one, exceptions being English and Scottish peers, Irish representative peers, the clergy of the Church of England, of the Church of Scotland and of the Roman Catholic Church, Government servants and contractors, and a few other obvious classes. All members receive a salary of £1000 per annum and travelling allowances. Members cannot resign their seats except by a rather roundabout way. No member may hold an office of profit under the Crown without seeking re-election (this does not apply now to appointments as Ministers), so that one way of resigning a seat is to apply either for the Stewardship of the Chiltern Hundreds, an ancient office for the suppression of brigands in the forest of that area, or for the Stewardship of Northstead. It is difficult to resign except by means of such a pleasant fiction as this, but it is quite impossible for a constituency to get rid of its member before the next election, even if he neglects his duties, or loses the confidence of his constituents, or changes his political opinions.

Elections are now governed by the Representation of the People Act, 1948. As far as possible the electoral areas are arranged so that there is one member to every 70,000 of the population. The areas consequently vary in size, as will be seen by reference to the map on p. 33. The franchise, or the right to vote, is based on the same conditions as those for local elections described on p. 76. In 1945 the number of voters in England and Wales was nearly 29,000,000. Before 1832 it was about 500,000. Up to that date there had been practically no change in the method of representation since the Restoration; the result was that the country was very unequally represented. Towns like Birmingham and Manchester with populations of over 100,000 were not represented as such. The hamlet of Bosseney in Cornwall consisted of three cottages and returned two members. Voting in those days was by open declaration, and consequently it was possible to know exactly how each man voted, and landlords were quite unscrupulous in bribing and intimidating those who were their tenants and had votes. It was not until 1872 that Parliament decided that the ballot should be secret. For an account of an old-style election, the reader should turn to Stanley Weyman's novel *Chippinge*.

The franchise has been extended gradually since 1832. At each stage an additional section of the community has been called upon to exercise the right to elect representatives; although many demanded a more speedy extension of the franchise, this less radical method has probably resulted in greater stability. The 1832 Act brought in about half a million of the upper middle classes and rearranged the constituencies more evenly. The Act of 1867 enfranchised some millions of the lower middle classes, especially in the towns, and that of 1884 made a uniform system in Boroughs and Counties. The basis of all these Acts was property, either in ownership or in use. Age and residence were first adopted as qualifications in 1918, and at the same time the franchise was extended to women over 30 years of age. Ten years later men and women were placed on an equality.

The Act of 1948 was based on the principle of "one man (or woman), one vote" and special franchises, such as the

University vote, were abolished. The qualifications were made the same for local as for Parliamentary elections, and similar provisions are made for absent and physically handicapped electors (see p. 76). Each constituency returns one member. The total number of members for Great Britain is 614; Northern Ireland (which has its own Parliament) returns twelve members to Westminster.

The position of a member of Parliament is rightly regarded as one of honour, but it also entails considerable responsibilities if he takes his duties seriously, and it is the rare exception for a member to do otherwise. With the broadening of the scope of government, the work of a member has increased considerably. Until well into this century the annual Parliamentary Session (brought to an end by a Prorogation) was from February to August, with autumn sittings if necessary; to-day the Session begins in the autumn and lasts until the following July or August with adjournments of short periods at Bank Holiday times. The House of Commons meets at 2.30 p.m. and sits until 10.30 p.m. and sometimes later. All-night sittings are not unknown. The fact that a member does not sit in the Chamber during the whole of that time does not mean that he is neglecting his duties. He has a vast correspondence with his constituents; he has reports and other documents to study; his morning is probably spent in Committees; even week-ends may be occupied with visits to his constituency for interviews and meetings. It is a full life and allows little time for relaxation.

It is important to understand the relation between a member and his constituency. He is generally elected not so much on his personal merits, great as they may be, as on his Party membership, but once he is elected he is something bigger than the representative of his supporters, or even of all his constituents. This point was expressed in a famous statement made by Edmund Burke when he was elected for Bristol in 1774.

To deliver an opinion is the right of all men; that of constituents is a weighty and respectable opinion, which a representative ought always to rejoice to hear; and which he ought always most seriously to consider. But *authoritative* instructions; *mandates* issued, which the member is bound blindly and implicitly to obey, to vote, and to argue for, though contrary to the clearest conviction of his judgment and conscience—these are things utterly unknown to the laws of this land, and which arise from a fundamental mistake of the whole order and tenor of our constitution. Parliament is not a *congress* of ambassadors from different and hostile interests; which interests each must maintain, as an agent and advocate, against other agents and advocates; but parliament is a *deliberative* assembly of *one* nation, with *one* interest, that of the whole; where, not local purposes, not local prejudices, ought to guide, but the general good, resulting from the general reason of the whole. You choose a member indeed; but when you have chosen him, he is not member of Bristol, but he is a member of *parliament*.

CHAPTER XII

# THE PARTY SYSTEM

It is inevitable that people with similar views on politics, or indeed on any matters, should tend to get together in order to gain strength by union in the furtherance of their principles. It is easy to see defects in our Party system, but during normal times it is probable that our public affairs will continue to be conducted by the democratic method of discussion between Parties. A fundamental principle of our way of government is that while the Party having a majority shall have the power to govern, the Party in the minority shall have equal rights of criticism. This would not be an unfair definition of the meaning of 'Democratic Government'. In abnormal circumstances some modification of the Party system may be desirable, and our constitution is loose enough to adjust itself to meet special conditions. Thus Ministries were formed during the two World Wars of members of all Parties.

The formation of Parties is not only inevitable but is of definite value. They help through their organisations to educate opinion, and they supply organised criticism which is a necessity for sound government.

The Party system in this country is bound up with the Cabinet system. The pressure of business on Parliament is so great that if there were no Party organisation at all it would be impossible to get even as much done as is achieved now, but the fact that the Cabinet represents the majority does mean that business goes forward and that most problems are faced and not left alone. There is, of course, a great danger in a Party having an absolute majority in the House of Commons. Even if it represents the general political temper of the country, the fact that it is almost unfettered may lead to alarmist legislation. This is where the value of a Second Chamber is felt. Our House of Lords is a constant factor, while the House of Commons is a changing factor, and the limited restraint which the Upper House can exercise has undoubtedly the effect of preventing precipitate legislation.

It would be foolish to ignore the influence of public opinion outside Parliament, and of opposition opinion within. Every Government knows that sooner or later it has to face the electors, and to flout public opinion is to invite defeat at the poll. Almost every Act of Parliament includes modifications and improvements suggested by the Opposition, or as a result of public opinion expressed in the newspapers, by public meetings or through deputations. The fact that the Opposition of to-day may be the Government of the future, has a restraining influence on extremists.

There have been for practically 200 years two main Parties in this country, with often a third small Party which is either a former Party in decay or a new Party in the process of building its strength. It is usual to date the rise of the Party system in its present form from the Restoration, and the Whigs and Tories of that period roughly corresponded to the Puritan and Royalist Parties. The Tory Party was mainly agricultural and was suspected after 1688 of Jacobite leanings. The Whig Party inherited the principles of the Commonwealth and was the strongest supporter of the 1688 settlement. It was not until 1780 that the Tory Party had any lengthy period of ascendancy, and then for some fifty years it was in power, a period covering the critical time of the French Revolution and of the Napoleonic Wars. From 1830 to 1874, with two short intervals, the Whig Party was in power. By the middle of the century the Tories had acquired the name of Conservatives and the Whigs were Radicals and Liberals.

The heyday of the Liberal Party began in 1905 when, it is significant to note, the Labour Party first gained a firm footing in the House of Commons with thirty members. By the end of the first World War the Liberal Party was split into rival factions and has never regained its old position as one of the two main Parties, a place that has been taken by the Labour Party. The economic crisis of 1931 gave the National Government (predominantly Conservative) a record majority of 425. Subsequent events showed the dangers of such overwhelming power; some members were inclined to take their duties lightly, and the smallness of the Opposition meant that criticism could not be maintained. Experience has shown that our system is most effective when a Government has a working majority and has to face the fire of an Opposition that includes former Ministers.

The election of 1945 illustrates the point previously made (see p. 111); a candidate receives votes as the representative of a Party; his personal qualities may sway a few hundred electors, but most people want a particular type of policy (as set out by one of the Parties) adopted, and they know this can only be done if that Party gains a majority and can form a Ministry. Sometimes opinion in a constituency may be evenly balanced (in 1945 there were four members whose majorities were 4, 6, 10 and 15 respectively) and then the personal factor may be decisive. Many were surprised, and some foreigners were startled, that Mr Winston Churchill did not become Prime Minister in 1945; but the electors could only vote for him by giving his Party a majority and this they were not prepared to do as they lacked confidence in it.

Our method of election is often criticised as producing results that are not strictly proportionate to the votes cast throughout the country. The figures for the elections of 1935 and 1945 will illustrate the point.

| | 1935 | | 1945 | |
|---|---|---|---|---|
| | Total votes | Seats | Total votes | Seats |
| Conservative | 10,488,626 | 387 | 8,693,858 | 189 |
| Labour | 8,325,260 | 154 | 11,985,733 | 393 |
| Liberal | 1,377,962 | 17 | 2,253,197 | 12 |

If these figures are studied carefully it will be seen that the number of seats won by each Party is not in proportion to the votes given, and in both cases the Government did not have an absolute majority in the country reckoned by total votes cast. (The votes given to Independents and some small Parties are not included in the above table.) An Opposition makes great play with this fact, but is always content to become the Government on the same terms! Another convention of the Party system is that the Opposition claims to speak for the nation and accuses the Government of acting in the interests of Party politics, or, in other words, the Government is doing what it was sent there to do, namely, to carry out the programme of the Party it represents.

Various suggestions have been made for securing a more representative Parliament. One method is known as the Alternative Vote; the elector marks on his voting paper the order of his preference, 1, 2, 3, etc. If no candidate gains an absolute majority over the others, then the first preferences given for the lowest candidate are ignored and the second preferences of those who put him first are added to the votes of the others.

A second method (too complicated to describe here) suggested is Proportional Representation; this would mean larger constituencies and at least three candidates. It is felt that constituencies are already too large for members to keep in touch with the electors, especially in county areas.

Little enthusiasm is shown amongst electors for either suggestion. They find that our present system, whatever its mathematical shortcomings may be, works in practice and does ensure that the Government can govern. The safeguard —and it is important to keep this in mind—is that the Government has to come before the electorate within five years at most of its accession to office, and that is a sobering influence on all Ministers as well as on members.

It would be difficult, if not impossible, to say why we have kept to the two-party system; this has not ruled out small third parties or dissident groups. We can see how, in some countries, a multiplicity of parties has led to much intrigue to form coalition and 'blocs', and has resulted in frequent changes of Ministries and a lack of stability. 'It works' is perhaps the only answer.

The organisation of the Parties in the constituencies dates back to the considerable extension of the franchise in 1867. The Conservatives were first in this field and in 1870 Disraeli set up the Central Conservative Office. The Liberals were not far behind. As we have already seen, the Labour Party came much later (see p. 17). These organisations have done much to educate public opinion on political questions through local meetings, the publication of pamphlets and by other forms of propaganda. All of them have failed to solve the problem of keeping local branches active between elections.

Inside Parliament the Parties are also organised. The leader of the Parliamentary Party is usually either the Prime Minister or the Leader of the Opposition. The officials responsible for the organisation are known as Whips, and those for the Government hold positions at the Treasury or in the Royal Household. The Chief Whip is largely concerned with planning the business of the House and takes into consideration the wishes of the Opposition whose Whips he consults. A certain amount of give and take is needed to ensure smooth working so that the Opposition and 'back benchers' (those not Ministers or ex-Ministers) feel that they are getting due consideration. This consultation 'through the usual channels' is sometimes misunderstood by strangers; it is part of the determination shared by all Parties to make the system workable and to let the Government govern and the Opposition oppose. The Whips also make sure that members are present at divisions (when votes are taken) in the House. This becomes a particularly difficult task when the numbers of the Parties are fairly even, as the absence or attendance of a few members may mean the defeat or success of the Government. A member who has to be absent pairs himself off with a member of another Party who also wishes to be absent, so that their votes cancel each other. When a division is expected the Chief Whip sends round a notice to the members of his Party warning them that their presence will be required, and these messages are underlined according to the importance of the occasion. A five-line Whip, as it is called, is an indication that the division will be a critical one. The following is an example of such a message:

> MOST IMPORTANT
>
> The Debate on the Second Reading of
>
> THE BILL
>
> will be concluded and a Division may be taken. Your Attendance not later than — o'clock is essential.
>
> Signed ——
>
> Chief Whip.

Party discipline is strict and this raises a question of first importance. Before the modern organisation of Parties a member felt at liberty to vote according to his own convictions unless, of course, he was the nominee of the owner or controller of a Borough, though as his principles would be similar to those of his Party he would normally vote with it, but it was not felt to be an act of disloyalty to vote otherwise when he felt constrained to do so. Nowadays there seems to be less room for a member to use his own judgment, and he is constrained to follow the behests of his Whip. Should he vote against his Party he runs the risk of not being nominated by them at the next election, and this would be a serious matter in most cases, as the Party Executive would put someone else up in his place. The Labour Party has a standing order that "Any Member who has conscientious scruples on any matter of Party policy shall be free to abstain from voting". This meets most difficulties.

Some men who could do inestimable service to the State in Parliament are undoubtedly prevented from rendering that service because they are not prepared to sacrifice their own judgment on all occasions to that of the Party, though quite prepared to support one or other on general principles. Regrettable as their exclusion may be, it is certain that a 'free-for-all' method of doing Parliamentary business would soon end in chaos and a collapse of democratic government.

CHAPTER XIII

# PARLIAMENT AT WORK

The simplest way of getting an idea of how the work of Parliament is done is to look through some full reports of the proceedings (see p. 164). Naturally no one day's report will illustrate all the methods of working, so that it will be necessary to study carefully several reports in order to get a complete view of things. The following description is based on several reports which have been chosen as typical examples of procedure.

The House of Lords report begins, "*The House met at half past two of the clock, the Lord Chancellor on the Woolsack*". It has already been pointed out that the Lord Chancellor acts as Speaker of the House of Lords (see p. 101).

After prayers a number of questions were asked; rather more latitude is allowed in the Lords than in the Commons in allowing explanations by the inquirers. Then followed the second reading debate on an Agricultural Bill. A Bill is the draft proposal for legislation; when it has passed both Houses and received the Royal Assent it becomes an Act of Parliament. This was a Bill which had passed through the House of Commons, where it had had the usual Third Reading. The First Reading is seldom more than receiving permission from the House for the Bill to be printed. The Second Reading is generally confined to a discussion on the main principles involved and details are not considered. If the Bill passes its Second Reading it goes through the Committee Stage, when each clause and often each phrase is discussed in detail. When the Bill has passed through the Committee Stage it reaches the Report Stage, when it is again presented to the House in its amended form. It is then read for the third time, and if accepted goes to the Upper House, where it goes through a similar procedure. The Lords' debate on this particular Bill dealt with the main principles of the Bill. The Second Reading was moved by the Parliamentary Secretary to the Ministry of Agriculture, one of the Government members of the House of Lords. After his speech the rejection was moved by one of the Opposition peers. A general discussion then followed, in the course of which one of the speakers pointed out that 23 of the 26 clauses in the Bill dealt with finance and consequently if the House tampered with these the Speaker would rule that their amendments infringed the privilege of the House of Commons. He therefore suggested that they should reject the Bill on the Second Reading and not waste time going into Committee when they knew that their amendments would not be accepted. At this point the debate was adjourned until the next day. A second Bill then passed the Report Stage. Another was read for the third time and passed, and a third was brought up from the Commons and read a first time. The report concludes, "House adjourned at ten minutes past five o'clock".

The report on the proceedings in the House of Commons begins, "*The House met at Half-past Two o'Clock.* PRAYERS [MR SPEAKER *in the Chair*]". The position of Speaker is one of the most honoured in the country. The first to bear the title was Sir Thomas Hungerford in 1377. In those days he was the representative of the House of Commons and its official spokesman in dealings with the King and the House of Lords. The Speaker is elected at the opening of each Parliament and serves as long as the Parliament lasts. Once he has been appointed he is now generally re-elected for as long as he cares to serve. He is usually chosen from amongst the supporters of the Government, but there is a long and healthy tradition that the Speaker is non-partisan. His duties are difficult and delicate. He has to decide who shall address the House. There is no accepted method by which he does this. A member has to "catch the Speaker's eye", but it takes a good deal of experience to know how this is accomplished. The general principle that guides him is that all Parties should be represented in the debate and that anyone with special knowledge of the subject under discussion should have an opportunity to speak. Although he has control over who shall speak, he has no means of stopping a member once he has started a speech, provided he keeps to the subject. Members have adopted various means of trying to persuade an over-loquacious speaker to stop. At one time it was customary to use cat-calls and other rude noises to indicate displeasure. On one occasion when this was being tried, the member who was speaking said, "If you do not allow me to finish my speech in my own way, I will not leave off at all", and this threat was sufficient to produce complete silence from his unwilling audience.

The Speaker also has to preserve the dignity of the House, to warn disorderly members and if necessary suspend them. He decides points of order and has, of course, an expert knowledge of the procedure of the House of Commons. This in itself is no light undertaking, but his ruling is accepted as final.

The slightest disrespect to the Speaker is now regarded as an insult to the House. It has not always been so. Records of the seventeenth century tell us that on one occasion a member "in a loud and violent manner, and, contrary to the usage of Parliament, standing near the Speaker's Chair, cried 'Baw' in the Speaker's ear, to the great terror and affrightment of the Speaker and of the members of the House".

The proceedings open with prayer and the reading of the sixty-seventh Psalm, "God be merciful unto us". This opening ceremony retains many relics of ancient practices. The House of Commons originally sat in the Chapter House of Westminster Abbey, but from 1547 it used St Stephen's Chapel in the Palace of Westminster. This explains why the House is still arranged with benches facing each other as though on both sides of an aisle. This fortuitous arrangement has helped to strengthen the idea of two main parties. When the structure of the new House of Commons (the 1850 building was destroyed in 1941) was under discussion it was decided to retain the old arrangement. Mr Winston Churchill then said, "The essence of good House of Commons speaking is the conversational style, the facility for quick informal interruption and interchange; haranguing from a rostrum would be a bad substitute". When prayers are ended the Mace is placed upon a table, and provided forty members are present the doorkeeper shouts, "Mr Speaker at the Chair", and the day's business can be opened. At any time if a 'Count' is made and less than forty members are present, the sitting ends.

On this particular day the first business was the presentation of a petition on behalf of the Trustees of the British Museum for their usual financial aid from Parliament. Following this a member moved that a new writ be issued for the election of a member in place of one who had recently died. A Writ of Election is issued by the Crown Office to the Returning Officer of the constituency, empowering him to arrange for an election.

Then followed the period for questions. Any member may ask questions provided that he gives one day's notice and does not ask more than three in one day. Only an hour is allowed for questions, and it is quite impracticable to give oral answers to all the questions that could be asked, so those which cannot be dealt with on the floor of the House are answered in the printed proceedings. This question time gives every member an opportunity for getting information or for raising matters which otherwise could not be dealt with in the House. It would be difficult to overestimate the value of this daily question time as a means of expressing public feeling and of keeping Ministries 'on their toes'. The information in the replies is supplied by the departments to the Ministers, and members may ask supplementary questions arising out of the answers if they so desire. For convenience questions are grouped so that Ministers can answer those referring to their departments on certain days of the week. On two consecutive days such subjects as the following were raised: pedestrian crossings, machine tools, taxicabs, the statue of General Gordon, Ruhr industries, the Brussels Treaty, feeding-stuffs for poultry, playing fields, Christmas puddings, rice, drill halls for Territorials, widows' pensions, tourist currency allowance, and the importation of monkeys.

After the question hour a new member was introduced by two other members. Each new member has to take the oath (or make an affirmation), sign the Test Roll, and be presented to the Speaker. The oath is, "I swear by Almighty God that I will be faithful and bear true allegiance to His Majesty King George and to his heirs and successors according to Law, so help me God". After this new member had been introduced and had taken his seat a member introduced a Private Member's Bill and he was given permission to have it printed. It is most important to distinguish between the different kinds of Bills. A *Public Bill* is a Government measure affecting the whole country. A *Private Bill* is one dealing with the affairs of a Corporation or some other body or particular person. A *Private Member's Bill* is introduced, not by the Government, but by some other member of the House. All Bills have to go through the same procedure, as detailed above. Private Members' Bills can be introduced on Fridays (when the House assembles at 11 a.m.) provided Government business allows. In the 1949 session such Bills were introduced for: Amending Law of Adoption, Prohibition of Hunting and Coursing, Spelling Reform, Censorship of Plays, Law Reform, and Docking and Nicking of Horses.

The report of this particular day's proceedings continues, "The House went into Committee of Supply on the Civil estimates". This calls for some explanation. The House of Commons in order to facilitate business has a number of committees which deal with special matters or with the Committee Stage of a Bill. The chief committees are: (1) *The Committee of the Whole House.* This is presided over by the Chairman of Committees or his deputy and not by the Speaker, and the proceedings are rather less formal than in the House. When its business is finished the committee rises, the Speaker returns to the chair and the House is once more in session. When the business relates to the expenditure of money it is known as a Committee of Supply: when it deals with the revenue it becomes a Committee of Ways and Means. (2) *Select Committees.* These consist of about fifteen members who are appointed to investigate some definite matter at the request of the House. There are a number of these committees from time to time and they usually sit in the mornings when the House is not in session. Such a committee may be concerned with the consideration of a Bill, or may be appointed to carry out some special investigation, as the recent Select Committee on Capital Punishment. (3) *Standing Committees* of forty to sixty members, chosen in proportion to the strengths of the Parties in the House. These committees deal with Bills which have been read but which often are of a very technical nature and need thorough investigation. Such committees sit during the mornings.

The Committee of Supply on this occasion was considering a supplementary vote on the civil estimates; that is to say, additional money required for the expenses of the House of Commons which had not been allowed for in the original estimates. After some discussion the votes were agreed to, the figures for one being 224 votes to 67, showing a majority of 157. This shows that there was a total attendance of 291 members out of 615. But this does not mean that these members were in the House throughout the debate, and this raises the interesting question of how the voting is done. At the end of a debate the Speaker (or Chairman, in committee) puts the motion and says, "As many of you as are of that opinion will say 'Aye'". When the supporters have shouted their 'Ayes', the Speaker says, "The contrary, 'No'", and another shout goes up. The Speaker then says, "I think the Ayes (or Noes) have it", and if his decision is not challenged the motion is accepted or rejected. If, however, his decision is challenged by anyone in the House, the order "Clear the Lobby" is given, bells are rung in every room and corridor, the policemen call out "Division", and members begin to arrive in the House from the library, from the dining room, or from wherever they may happen to have been. After two minutes the Speaker again puts the question and this time the members pass out of the House. They go through one or other of the two division lobbies, the Aye division being on the Speaker's right and the No division on his left. As they pass through their names are recorded and they are counted by the Tellers. When the members have finished passing through, the Tellers walk up to the table on which the Mace lies, bow to the Speaker, and the one representing the majority vote announces the result. The House adjourns at 10.30 p.m., but it frequently decides to continue after that time either to conclude important business or for what is called an Adjournment Debate when any member may raise subjects for general discussion after having given notice. During one week the following subjects were raised on the adjournment: historic houses, transport, opencast coalmining, Spain, expulsion of a British subject from Hungary, and electricity supplies.

At the end of the proceedings the doorkeeper steps into the lobby and cries out "Who goes home?" The cry is taken up by the policemen and other attendants, and this is an indication that the sitting for the day is over. As the members go out the attendants say to them, "The usual time to-morrow, Sir, the usual time to-morrow". Both these remarks are relics of old days. When there were dangers of footpads and other rogues for those who ventured abroad at night in Westminster and London, Yeomen of the Guard escorted members home if they wished it and the call "Who goes home?" was a means of collecting parties together, and the call is still used as a sign of the end of the day's work in the House of Commons.

Up to 1882 there were no means available for bringing a sitting to an end if members wilfully prolonged the debate. At that period the Irish Party was determined to obstruct the business of the House until Irish affairs were settled to their satisfaction. They adopted the method of speaking in turn as long as possible; this needed some skill to avoid being irrelevant and so being checked by the Speaker. This must not be confused with the filibustering practised in the United States Congress; a member can there talk on anything, even read aloud, until he is physically exhausted. The historic example of obstruction in the House of Commons took place on 31 January 1881. The debate on the Coercion Act was kept going by the Irish members for forty-one hours! Everyone was in despair. At length Speaker Brand decided that it was his duty to extricate the House from the difficulty by closing the debate on his own authority. When his action was challenged he replied that he had acted from a sense of duty to the House.

This incident and later difficulties resulted in the adoption of three methods of closure. The simplest method is when any member proposes that "the question be now put". If at least one hundred members vote in favour of this motion and have a majority, a division is called. The second method is known as the 'Guillotine'. A motion is made that at a stated hour on a stated day all questions, whether debated or not, shall be put to the House. A third method (seldom used) is known as the 'Kangaroo' closure; by this the House authorises the Chairman to pick out from the long series of amendments submitted those he considers to be essential; these only are debated. Naturally the Opposition always complains bitterly of the use of these drastic methods of getting through the business; but every Government finds it necessary to adopt them, however much it may have talked of autocratic methods when on the opposite bench!

Public questions arise from time to time which call for thorough investigation. A Statutory Commission is then appointed by the Government in consultation with the leaders of other parties. Such a Commission receives a Royal Warrant to carry out its work: a Report (one of many Blue Books) is eventually issued, making definite suggestions which may or may not be adopted by the Government.

CHAPTER XIV

# NATIONAL CONTROL AND OWNERSHIP

Parliament makes grants to a number of institutions and organisations and thereby accepts a measure of responsibility for their activities; such grants are subject to review by the Commons just as any other part of the national expenditure may be discussed. A grant is made, for instance, to the Universities; in 1946–7 this amounted to nearly seven million pounds; in theory, and quite legally, Parliament could lay down any terms it likes for the continuation of that grant; in practice the Universities are left unhampered by Government interference. If the Universities were to slip back into the lazy ways of the eighteenth century Parliament would doubtless, and rightly, step in; but provided the Universities carry out their functions to general satisfaction, it is most unlikely that they would be troubled by any Government regulations. This is another example of how we do not enforce or even use powers that are in existence; there are unwritten understandings and conventions in every part of our constitution that are in keeping with the national tradition of being satisfied with a good working scheme based on trust rather than insisting on a rigid system that would allow little or no play for the individual or corporate initiative.

## i. *State Control*

In this chapter we shall review some of the many forms of control and ownership exercised by the community. No simple classification is possible as the degree of control varies from instance to instance. During this century there has been a growing tendency for the Government (of whatever Party) to give aid to essential industries or to cultural institutions either by grants or subsidies. Since 1945 this has gone further, and actual ownership by the State ('nationalisation') is considered better in some cases than the granting of financial assistance.

Two examples of Government support for otherwise autonomous organisations will illustrate the simplest form of grant.

During the 1939–45 war a Council for the Encouragement of Music and the Arts (C.E.M.A.) was set up to organise concerts of good music, performances of the best plays and exhibitions of pictures in towns and villages where such pleasures were almost unknown. In the most remote places the response was astonishing and proved beyond doubt that if people are given the opportunity they appreciate literature, art and music of the highest quality. It was felt that this excellent project should not die with the end of the war, and so C.E.M.A. became the Arts Council of Great Britain with the support of the Ministry of Education.

Our second example is provided by the British Council, which was formed in 1934 for the purpose of spreading a knowledge of British culture in foreign countries. The method is to establish a British Institute in the capital of a country; this becomes a centre for organising lectures on literature, the arts and British institutions; exhibitions of pictures are arranged and language courses provided. There has been some severe criticism in Parliament at times of the work of the British Council on the grounds that it gave too much prominence to 'upper class' points of view. Such criticism usually bears fruit and in this way undesirable tendencies are kept in check.

The British Broadcasting Corporation is an example of a Public Corporation operating under a Royal Charter granted for five-year periods. Its income is derived from receiving and television licences and from special grants for the Overseas and European Services. The Government appoints the Chairman, Vice-Chairman and the Governors, but does not interfere with the day-to-day running of the programmes nor with the general policy. At times there are complaints that the B.B.C. is too favourable to one Party or the other, but these criticisms tend to cancel out. There is no attempt to broadcast political propaganda of a one-party character; the free play of opinion is permitted within the limits laid down by the Governors and not by the Government. The accounts are presented annually and provide an opportunity for discussion in the Commons when members enjoy airing their own likes and dislikes of the contents of the programmes. A more thorough review of the B.B.C. is made when the Charter comes up for renewal; the Government may then set up a Committee or Commission to study the working and policy of the B.B.C. In most countries broadcasting is done by private companies who make their profits out of fees received from commercial companies for advertising; we are happily spared exhortations to buy someone's face powder after listening to a symphony concert.

Another type of control is represented by the Central Electricity Board set up in 1926 to co-ordinate the work of the many companies (some municipal and others private) supplying electricity. Main transmission lines (the grid) were established so that there should be more uniformity of supply.

A greater degree of State control is illustrated by the London Passenger Transport Board established in 1933 by Act of Parliament. Traffic conditions in London had become almost chaotic owing to competition between rival bus companies and the lack of any over-all supervision of all means of transport. The Board is a Public Corporation; holders of stock in the private companies were compensated either by purchase or by receiving new stock at fixed rates of interest. The L.P.T.B. is a commercial undertaking that has to pay its own way.

## ii. *State Ownership*

Complete State ownership is not a new device. There was, for instance, a proposal in 1830 that the Government should build main line railways, but the Cabinet declined the suggestion, it is said, on the advice of the Duke of Wellington who was Prime Minister; he did not like railways. It is interesting to note that Gladstone's Railway Act of 1844 reserved the right of State intervention and the option of purchase. This Act also stipulated that at least one train a day should be run on every line at a charge of a penny a mile for the convenience of short-distance passengers. (These were the 'Parliamentary trains' of *The Mikado.*) During the two World Wars, the Government took over the control of the railways, and in 1947 an Act was passed nationalising railways and canals.

The best example of a national service or monopoly that has developed from small beginnings (without any vision of the outcome) is provided by the Post Office. This can be traced back to the royal couriers of medieval times. Out of this service developed the provision of regular 'mails of letters' (or bags) for the convenience of private persons. Mail coaches with armed guards were run in the eighteenth century. There were also arrangements for sending letters abroad or to the colonies by packet-boats. The modern period begins in 1840 with the introduction of the penny post and the postage stamp, both the result of suggestions by Sir Rowland Hill (1795–1879). Up to then postage had been paid by the recipient according to distance; a single-sheet letter from London to Edinburgh cost 1*s.* 4½*d.* By Sir Rowland Hill's scheme the sender paid the postage of one penny for half-an-ounce and affixed a stamp in proof of payment. The era of the penny post lasted from 1840 to 1922. Gradually the Post Office extended its services. The Savings Bank was opened in 1861; the telegraph services were purchased in 1870, the year in which postcards were first used. Postal orders were introduced in 1881 and a parcel service two years later. In 1905 the Post Office bought out the National Telephone Company. Cables and Wireless were nationalised in 1947. The Post Office is the Government agent for the collection of many licence fees and for the payment of family allowances and pensions.

From the story of the Post Office it can be seen that the action of the State in taking over services of public importance has over a century's history behind it. We are also accustomed to municipalities owning such services as trams, buses, electricity and gas. In 1946 there were 370 municipal and 190 private electricity undertakings; these were all nationalised in 1947; in the following year all gas companies were nationalised.

Such measures of nationalisation of public utility services do not excite much opposition; better distribution should result from central co-ordination and thus even remote hamlets may hope to have the advantages that have hitherto been almost entirely town monopolies. Thus the grid may pass close to a village, but the high cost of connecting up has made it out of the question for cottagers. By spreading costs and charges it is hoped to extend all such benefits.

Far more controversial is the nationalisation of industries that have hitherto been owned by private companies. It is not easy to draw a line in this matter; for instance, coal is a necessity of general use; should it be classed as private industry or as a public utility service? What about milk and bread? The Milk Marketing Board is a form of control, and subsidies or rationing can be used to regulate supplies, prices, and distribution. Discussion of the principles underlying these problems is beyond the scope of this book, but it is worth noting the method of administration of one such scheme.

On 1 January 1947 the ownership of the coal-mines was transferred to the nation. Special circumstances and past history removed most objections to this course. During this century the coal industry has often been in difficulties, and several attempts have been made to find a solution. Royal Commissions have investigated the problem. Subsidies have been paid by the Government to tide over bad times. The miners themselves were determined to get the mines nationalised, and this method, which had been proposed by one Commission, was finally adopted. Under the Act of 1946 a National Coal Board was set up and the country divided into Regions each with its Board. The running of the industry was placed in their charge; it was not 'to be run from Whitehall', that is, by Civil Servants from a government office. The coal industry is expected to pay its own way. As a State monopoly it can command more capital than it could before nationalisation with which to bring its equipment up to date. Experience of this method will alone prove if it is the most workable and productive; a period of 'trial and error' is inevitable with such an unprecedented form of State responsibility.

As soon as the Coal Board and other bodies such as the Transport Commission were set up, an interesting problem arose in the House of Commons. Would questions on the working of such services and industries be allowed? The Government argued that the Ministers concerned were not responsible for day-to-day working, and that it was a matter of principle to leave the managements to get on with their jobs; only general policy on large issues could be the subject of questions. Members appealed to the Speaker. He had to take into account the fact that if questions of detail were allowed, such as "Why did the 10.30 arrive late?", the period allotted to questions in the House would have to be considerably extended. He therefore declined to give a decision straight away, and suggested that for a period they should all see how things went and he would consider questions on their merits before trying to lay down a ruling. The House was content to leave the problem in this indeterminate fashion; it illustrates once more our reluctance to bind ourselves by rigid rules; we prefer to see 'how it works', and to reach a practical solution by experience. Far more difficult than this matter of questions in the House, is how to combine public control and ownership with the encouragement of initiative amongst the workers. Time alone will show how far this is possible.

One danger calls for vigilance. The members of these powerful Boards are appointed by the Government; these are highly paid positions. The Chairman of the Coal Board has a salary of £8500 and each of the eight members receives £5000 a year. There is a temptation to appoint supporters of the Government and to regard these positions as awards for Party services. There is no reason to think that this is a likely development, but the danger is there and will need combatting. It would indeed be a tragedy if, having got rid of the old patronage and spoils system to be described in the next chapter, we fall victims to a new form of the old disease.

CHAPTER XV

# THE CIVIL SERVICE

The term 'Civil Servant' was first used in the eighteenth century by the East India Company for anyone employed by it who was not in its Army. Later the name came to be applied to all civilians in Government service.

## i. *Patronage*

The work of government has always required the services of full-time officials and clerks for administration—that is, to carry into practice the decisions made by the executive. As long as little was expected from the government beyond the defence of the realm and the preservation of law and order, the number of people employed on administration was small. Appointment was by nomination and patronage. It was a haphazard method that brought unequal results; some of the most efficient as well as some of the most inefficient public servants of the nineteenth century were appointed in this way. We have several times noted how during that century, and at a rapidly increasing rate during this century, the government has been expected to do more and more in trade, in health, in education and in promoting social betterment. This has meant vast increases in the numbers employed in the Civil Service.

One of the evils of the old system—if such it may be called—was that many positions had become sinecures; their original purpose had become obsolete, but the jobs were not abolished. For instance, Horace Walpole (1717–97), at the age of twenty-one, was provided by his father the Prime Minister with three places—Usher of the Exchequer, Comptroller of the Pipe, and Clerk of the Estreats (the very names suggest a world of fantasy) which together brought an annual income of £1200; and this the famous letter writer enjoyed for sixty years! The small amount of work was done by an indifferently paid clerk. Edmund Burke (1729–97) was the first statesman to attack this evil. In a speech in 1780 he said:

> To what end, Sir, does the office of *removing wardrobe* serve at all? Why should a *jewel office* exist for the sole purpose of taxing the king's gifts of plate?...Why should an office of the *robes* exist, when the *groom of the stole* is a sinecure, and that this is a proper object of his department?...For the payment of these useless establishments, there are no less than *three useless treasurers;* two to hold a purse, and one to play with a stick.

His suggestions for reform were coldly received.

The first stage in building up an efficient service was to get rid of such sinecure appointments that were not only an intolerable financial burden, but poisoned the whole administration by setting a wrong standard. This was a long process that meant fighting vested interests; the holders did not think in terms of public service but in terms of personal property, for that is how they regarded their positions.

The next stage was to make sure that those appointed to posts should have the requisite ability and knowledge. In face of public criticism a show was made of testing the qualifications of nominated candidates. An amusing instance of this in the year 1834 is given in the autobiography of Anthony Trollope, the novelist. He was nominated to a clerkship in the General Post Office by a friend of his mother.

He was examined as to his fitness by the assistant secretary.

> I was asked to copy some lines from *The Times* newspaper with an old quill pen, and at once made a series of blots and false spellings. "That won't do, you know."...I was then asked whether I was proficient in arithmetic. What could I say? I had never learned the multiplication table and had no more idea of the rule of three than of conic sections. "I know a little of it", I said humbly, whereupon I was sternly assured that on the morrow, should I succeed in showing that my handwriting was all that it ought to be, I should be examined as to that little of arithmetic.

So he went home and copied out carefully some pages from Gibbon and took them along with him to the office next morning. But when he got there "I was seated at a desk without any further reference to my competency". Trollope proved an excellent Civil Servant and was later entrusted with highly responsible duties.

The old order fought hard against any change; Trollope, for instance, strongly objected to any suggestion of competitive examination. The growing need for men of intelligence and knowledge would not however have been met under the former patronage method of appointment. The year 1853 is a landmark in the history of public administration. At the request of Gladstone, who was then Chancellor of the Exchequer, Sir Stafford Northcote and Sir Charles Trevelyan studied the problem and issued their report in that year. They recommended appointment by competitive examination under a central authority. There was strong opposition to this proposal; some asked if such a means could ensure the appointment of gentlemen; others, more pertinently, if an academic examination was the best way of testing ability for the work. In spite of this opposition, the Civil Service Commission was established in 1855, but at first only nominated candidates were tested. It took another fifteen years to get the principle of open competitive examination accepted by all departments except the Foreign Office; this was not the least of the services to the State rendered by Gladstone. Lord Morley summed up this achievement in these words:

> It was true to say of this change that it placed the whole educated intellect of the country at the service and disposal of the State, that it stimulated the acquisition of knowledge, and that it rescued some of the most important duties in the life of the nation from the narrow class to whom they had hitherto been confided.

## ii. *Present System*

There have been many changes in the system of examinations and of appointment since 1870. Different types of work have been distinguished, and the interview and other methods used to supplement the written examination.

The present scheme recognises four main classes:

(1) *Administrative*; the standard is that of a University degree;

(2) *Executive*; the examination is taken at the age of 18 to 18½;

(3) *Clerical*; the examination is taken at 16 to 17 years of age; and

(4) *Clerical assistants and typists*; for women only between the ages of 15 and 32.

These are not rigid divisions; promotion is possible not only within each class but from class to class, and the policy now is to make the scheme as flexible as possible so that talent can be more quickly recognised and rewarded.

It is a mistake to think of the Civil Service as being an entirely clerical body; such work does, of course, occupy many Civil Servants, but even amongst them there are degrees of responsibility, and the nature of the work is as varied as the range of the Ministries. There are also special classes that do not fit into the above scheme—such as tax inspectors, factory inspectors, and customs officers. Then there are the specialist appointments of lawyers, scientists, doctors, accountants, engineers and architects.

The Civil Servant has a good deal of criticism to suffer; he (or she) is a convenient person on whom to work off our irritation when things do not go as smoothly as we expect, or when yet another form has to be filled up. We murmur of 'red tape' and of delays and formalities. Such criticisms are sometimes merited, and it is important that we should not accept any inefficiency in the State administration. Civil Servants are as prone to human weaknesses as the rest of us—there may be a love of asserting authority, or perhaps a willingness to pass on decisions to others. Yet we regard their integrity as a matter of course. It is astonishing that out of such a shady past there has developed an administration with an unrivalled reputation for impartial and reliable service. This has been built up by the devotion of men of public spirit and sometimes of almost missionary zeal; even the days of patronage saw a Sir Edwin Chadwick (1801–90) who did fine work on the old Poor Law Commission, and the reorganised service brought in Sir Robert Morant (1863–1920) whose name will always be associated with the progress of education. It would be very easy to make a long list of distinguished Civil Servants who have made important contributions to the administration of the country, and to whom may be credited the initiative that has resulted in important reforms. Such initiative has not been of a political character, for it is important to understand the relation between Minister and Civil Servant.

Happily the 'spoils system' died out in this country with the replacement of patronage by open examination. When there is a change of Ministry there is not a corresponding change of officials in the departments; Ministers come and go, but the staff of a Ministry from the Permanent Secretary down to the newly appointed junior clerk remains unchanged except by promotion or retirement. All the accumulated knowledge and experience of the staff is at the disposal of the Minister whatever his political colour. A Civil Servant may detest the policy he has to put into action but he carries it out as carefully as if it were his own conception—that is the tradition.

Although the permanent staff of a Ministry cannot initiate legislation—that is the business of the Cabinet and the Minister concerned—it does provide the facts on which legislation is based, and it can warn Ministers of likely dangers or point out the lessons of experience. Some Acts owe much to the permanent officials; the Criminal Justice Act of 1948 is a good example as it embodied ideas that had been forming in the minds of officials based on the experience of the working of the law gained by such bodies as the Prison Commission. The Home Secretary had all this material at his disposal and took into consultation those experts in the Home Office whose suggestions naturally carried weight. The policy to be followed was laid down by the Cabinet on the advice of the Home Secretary. The subsequent Bill that was presented to Parliament was largely non-controversial, and all Parties combined to improve the original draft. This considerable measure of agreement did not exclude criticism. Not many Bills are of this character, but there is far more agreement on general principles in Parliament than the public is aware; mere obstruction is not in our tradition; all agree that the government must be carried on even if a large section disapproves of a particular Government. In the same way the members of the Civil Service loyally carry out their instructions however unpalatable the policy may be.

In addition to the Civil Service attached to the Ministries, there is the Local Government Service. Each authority has its own methods of recruitment, but many now follow the scheme suggested by a National Joint Council. The scope of the work is as wide and varied as in Government departments and offers opportunities for professional experts as well as for clerical workers.

CHAPTER XVI

# HOW IT IS ALL PAID FOR

On at least one day in the year we are all keenly interested in the proceedings of Parliament; this is the day when the Chancellor of the Exchequer makes his Budget statement, or surveys the nation's income and expenditure and announces changes in taxation. A 'budget' meant at one time a bag of papers; so we still speak of 'opening the budget'.

The Chancellor of the Exchequer is the head of the Treasury, which is the department that controls finances and so exercises a certain amount of restraint over all other departments. The Exchequer is the descendant of the Revenue Office of the time of the Normans. Twice a year the Sheriffs paid in the money they had collected to the Exchequer. The money was stored in great chests each guarded by three locks so that they could not be opened without the approval of the Teller, the Clerk and the Auditor. The name 'Exchequer' is derived from the table at which the Sheriffs handed over their money. The cloth on the table was divided into squares and coins were used as counters. The Sheriffs had wooden tallies, notched according to the sums of money with which they dealt.

Parliament's part in dealing with finance is to determine where the money is to come from, to vote the money for approved expenditure, and to see that it is properly spent.

It will be helpful to have before us lists containing the chief items of income and expenditure (pp. 143 and 144).

At the end of the year all Government departments prepare their estimates. These are submitted to the Treasury and if approved are then ready to be put before Parliament. The Treasury tries to persuade the departments to cut down their estimates as much as possible. During the first half of the year twenty days, not consecutive, are set aside for the House to go

*Main sources of income*, 1947–48

| | £ *million* |
|---|---|
| Inland Revenue: | |
| Income tax | 1189·7 |
| Surtax | 91·2 |
| Death duties | 172·0 |
| Stamp duties | 56·3 |
| Excess Profits Tax | 252·6 |
| Customs and Excise: | |
| Customs | 791·1 |
| Excise | 629·7 |
| Motor vehicle duties | 49·1 |
| Broadcast receiving licences | 11·2 |
| Crown lands | 1·0 |
| Receipts from sundry loans | 23·0 |
| Miscellaneous | 242·6 |
| Post Office | 143·3 |
| Income tax deducted from Excess Profits Tax post-war refunds | 23·2 |

into Committee of Supply to discuss these estimates. Votes on Account are also passed, which allow the departments to draw upon the Treasury for necessary expenditure until the Finance Act has been passed. It is important to notice that while members may criticise the various items of expenditure and can propose reductions, they cannot suggest increases, as all proposals for expenditure must come from the Crown, that is, the Ministry. When the estimates have been passed by the Committee of Supply, the Committee of Ways and Means then passes the necessary resolution for the money to be appropriated. Both these Committees are Committees of the Whole House.

Early in the Session, usually in April, the Chancellor of the Exchequer introduces the Budget. This has always been considered the greatest night of the year in Parliament since

*Main items of expenditure*, 1947–48

| | £ *million* |
|---|---|
| Interest on the National Debt | 500·9 |
| Defence: | |
| Army votes | 383·6 |
| Navy votes | 194·3 |
| Air votes | 181·9 |
| Ministry of Supply | 94·1 |
| Other civil votes: | |
| Central government and finance | 9·2 |
| Foreign and imperial | 59·1 |
| Home department, law and justice | 30·8 |
| Education and broadcasting | 182·1 |
| Health, housing, town planning, labour and national insurance | 379·6 |
| Trade, industry and transport | 170·0 |
| Common services (works, stationery, etc.) | 78·3 |
| Non-effective charges (pensions) | 91·2 |
| Exchequer contributions to local revenues, etc. | 66·4 |
| Supply, food and miscellaneous services | 702·4 |
| Post Office | 143·3 |

the days of William Pitt (1759–1806). In Gladstone's time the Budget speech was often five or six hours in length. Nowadays it is somewhat shorter but none the less important. By an Act passed in 1913 all variations in taxation come into force the day after the Budget speech. The Budget speech is followed by many debates and discussions on the contents of the subsequent Finance Act. An Appropriation Act is first passed which authorises all the grants for expenditure, and the Finance Act concludes the matter by reimposing taxes or making alterations in taxation.

A consideration of the sources of revenue raises one or two important points. Taxation is either direct or indirect. It is direct when it is paid by the individual to the taxation authorities, the income tax being the best example of this. Indirect taxation is when the taxes are passed on to others; for example a tax on tea is in the first instance paid by the importers, but the cost is always passed on to the consumer. It will be noticed that the largest source of revenue is from the income tax. This would have shocked Parliament a hundred years ago, as the tax was first imposed during the Napoleonic Wars as an emergency measure. In 1842 the income tax was 7*d.* in the pound on incomes over £150. Gladstone expressed the hope at one time that it would be possible to do away with the income tax. He little knew that in the year 1947 it would be 9*s.* in the pound. He would have been still more horrified to see the present size of the Budget, since in 1851 the revenue was £56,307,000 and the expenditure £53,581,000. In 1947 the total revenue was £3,459,639,000, and the expenditure £4,057,957,000. In 1907 a new principle was introduced of distinguishing between earned and unearned incomes in assessing the income tax. In 1909 the surtax was imposed, being an additional tax above the ordinary rates on incomes of over £2000. Various reliefs are allowed for earned income, for wife, children and other dependents, for life assurance, etc.

The difference between customs and excise is simply that customs are duties levied on imports, and excise is a duty charged on home goods, or a tax in the form of a licence to perform certain duties or sell certain articles. Typical items on which customs are levied are tea and tobacco; excise taxes are paid on such things as beer and matches, and licenses include the entertainments tax, guns, dogs, etc.

In the list of expenditure given above the first entry refers to the National Debt. This is a debt incurred usually during periods of stress, such as the Napoleonic Wars or the World Wars. In 1900 the debt was £765,216,000. After the 1914–18 war it rose to £7,875,642,000. The second World War brought it up to £25,734,200,000, an astronomical figure beyond our imaginations, but, unfortunately, a hard fact.

Part of this debt is funded, that is to say, there is no obligation to pay it off on any definite date; and the greater part is unfunded, that is, people who have invested money in Government Stocks or have bought National Savings Bonds or Certificates have only done so for a set period. Interest has to be paid on these loans we make to the Government and provision made for repayment of the principal. When the date for repayment comes due, it is sometimes possible to arrange a Conversion Loan on terms favourable enough for the holders to reinvest their money. William Pitt started a Sinking Fund in 1786 for the accumulation of money with which to pay off the capital. A definite sum is set on one side every year for this purpose. The National Debt is a huge charge. It will be noted that interest and management come to over £500,000,000 for 1947–48.

In discussing the development of Parliament it was pointed out what an important part the control of finance played in its history. One of the problems that we now have to face is whether the House of Commons really has sufficient control over finances. The estimates are drawn up by the departments, all the details of methods of taxation, etc., are settled by the Chancellor of the Exchequer and the Cabinet. As the Government supporters feel that they must support the proposals laid before the House, there is very little discussion of the methods of raising the revenue, or of the merit of the uses to which the revenue is to be put. Indeed during this century the House of Commons has never compelled the Cabinet to cut down its estimates. The House of Commons is too large an assembly for dealing with such an intricate subject. A Committee of over 600 members is not a working body when it comes to investigating very complicated figures. A National Expenditure Committee, representative of all Parties, does valuable work in studying accounts and pointing out how economies could be effected.

The formal motion which is sometimes put by the Opposition to decrease the salary of a Minister is merely a Parliamentary way of creating an opportunity for discussing the policy of his department. It is not primarily a method of criticising expenditure. Another difficulty is that we have got into the habit after two world wars of thinking in hundreds of millions, and consequently any small economies that could be made seem relatively so minute as not to be worth the making, and moreover each department firmly believes that it is working on the minimum sum of money and fights hard with the Treasury for keeping its estimates intact. Here is a problem that concerns each of us, for we have to pay the bills!

CHAPTER XVII

# THE LAW

The establishment of law and order is an essential condition for the peaceful development of any community whether it is a sports club or a nation. This is not simply a question of suppressing violence but of finding some way by which the members can settle differences between themselves. We can see this need in its early stages even as late as the nineteenth century. The pioneers of North America who went out West in search of new lands were beyond the reach of the central government; a community would therefore appoint a Judge and Sheriff from amongst themselves and form a body of Vigilantes to support this crude form of justice.

## i. *The King's Peace*

It would be an interesting task to trace the history of the establishment of the reign of law in this country. We should have to note the work of the local courts of the Shires and Hundreds in the early Middle Ages. Then it would be necessary to study the work of Henry II, one of our greatest kings; it was he who enforced the idea of the 'King's Peace'—the principle that a crime is a wrong against the community and not merely against an individual; he developed the system of itinerant royal justices and encouraged the use of juries. The attempts of his son John to override the new system led to Magna Carta (1215) which contained the clause:

> No freeman shall be taken or imprisoned or disseised [dispossessed] or exiled or in any way destroyed, nor will we go upon him nor will we send upon him except by the lawful judgment of his peers or the law of the land.

Another clause provided that right and justice should not be sold, denied, or delayed.

These clauses were to be used (not always in their original sense) during succeeding centuries as statements of fundamental principles of English law.

The work of Edward I would next need our attention with the gradual increase of the use and influence of Parliament. Our study would also lead us to the work of a long line of distinguished judges who established a high code of justice, sometimes in spite of royal opposition, and expounded the law for the benefit of their successors. The list would include Ranulf de Glanvil (d. 1190), Henry de Bracton (d. 1268), Sir Thomas Littleton (1422–81), Sir Edward Coke (1552–1634), Sir Matthew Hale (1609–76), and Sir William Blackstone (1723–80). So we should come to modern times with the system of courts as we know them. This long history is not ended; apart from new Acts of Parliament, changes are made from time to time in administration; thus the Criminal Justice Act of 1948 brought in a number of reforms based on accumulated experience.

It would not be an exaggeration to say that this history of the development of law and its administration is more important than the record of past political and military events. Unfortunately the history of law is not easy and colourful reading and there are technicalities which the layman finds difficult.

A deeply seated sense of justice and fair play is the most noticeable element in this history; no one can say how it originated for it can be traced back to the dim past. It is like a stream flowing through our history; at times it has gone underground and there have been flagrant acts of injustice, but it has come to the surface again with increased volume. This sense of justice is the greatest safeguard of our common rights as citizens.

## ii. *Principles*

Certain big principles in the administration of justice are now well established though each had to be won by determined struggle. Here are the most important:

1. *The judges are independent and irremovable.*

This was established after the Revolution of 1688 and is one of the most important (but often overlooked) results of that event. Judges are appointed for life and cannot be removed except for the gravest reasons, on an address presented to the King by both Houses of Parliament. They are in no way subject to pressure from the Government and maintain complete political impartiality. An interesting illustration of their position occurred in 1931 when, by the National Economy Act, the salaries of 'servants of the Crown' were reduced. When the Treasury proposed to apply this to the judges they protested, as it implied that they were under Government control.

2. *No one may be kept in custody without speedily being brought to trial.*

The Habeas Corpus Act of 1679 finally established this principle though it had been generally accepted for some time previously. The name is taken from two important words in the writ, "Thou shalt have the body (in court)". If anyone is imprisoned without being soon brought to trial, or before examining magistrates, he can appeal for a writ of Habeas Corpus so that he can be produced in court and a proper charge made against him. In times of national emergency the Act may be suspended.

3. *Trial must be in open court.*

Secret trials are repugnant to us just as we object to any use of 'third degree' methods by the police. In a few special types of case such as those in Juvenile Courts the public is not admitted but representatives of the Press are allowed with some limitations on the publication of names.

4. *For indictable offences, the accused (or defendant) has the right of trial by jury.*

It is difficult to give a simple definition of the term 'indictable', but as a rough guide it may be taken to mean offences liable to a penalty of more than three months' imprisonment. The business of the jury is to decide on the facts as brought out in evidence in court; their verdict must be a unanimous one of 'Guilty' or 'Not Guilty'; in Scotland a verdict of 'Not proven' is possible. It is for the judge to decide matters of law and to pronounce sentence; he must accept the verdict of the jury.

5. *It is for the prosecution to establish the case against the accused.*

Another way of putting this is to say that everyone is innocent until proved guilty. All facts must be established on evidence. Hearsay evidence is not admissible. In the case of *Bardell* v. *Pickwick* the judge said to Sam Weller, "You must not tell us what the soldier, or any other man said; it's not evidence". The accused is not obliged to give evidence in a criminal case, and if he is declared 'Not Guilty' he is discharged and he cannot again be accused of the same offence unless entirely new evidence is produced.

From this it can be seen that English law safeguards the rights of an accused person; this method may occasionally set free a guilty man or woman for want of conclusive evidence but it is better that a guilty person should sometimes escape than that innocent people should suffer. No human system is perfect and wrong convictions have been made, but their number is a minute fraction of the whole; it is equally true to say that many guilty people are never brought to trial because the evidence against them is not strong enough.

The law also helps the defendant, if he is poor, by providing counsel (a lawyer) under the Poor Persons Defence Act of 1903 and other assistance under the Legal Aid and Advice Act of 1949; this is some offset against the high costs of legal cases.

There are three sources of law in England: Common Law, Statute Law, and Equity. We need not trouble about the last as it is now mostly covered by the other two; it originated in petitions to the King for justice in cases that could not be dealt with by normal legal means.

*Common Law.* We are now so accustomed to thinking of laws as Acts of Parliament that we may find it difficult to grasp the meaning and significance of the Common Law. It is sometimes described as "The Universal Custom of the Realm"; long before laws (statutes) were written down it was necessary to do justice. It was, and is, the business of a judge to 'do right' in any case brought before him; he had to use his own sense of justice and to compare the case with others he had met or with which his fellow judges had dealt. So there grew up a body of precedents or previous decisions which became a guide in later cases. This 'Custom of the Realm' was the basis of justice long before Parliament began making laws, and although Parliamentary legislation now covers a far wider field than in the Middle Ages there are still occasions when the Common Law is the only resource. This Common Law is perhaps the greatest heritage that the United States of America has received from England, and it has also had considerable influence in other countries.

*Statute Law.* This is the law as enacted by the King in Parliament; every year it grows in bulk as the Government extends its control over more and more of the community life. So considerable has this extension become that the House of Commons cannot discuss the details of all legislation. An Act will therefore frequently give the responsible Minister the power to issue detailed regulations and orders that have the force of law. The number of such regulations increases from year to year. While no one suggests that this method of 'delegated legislation', as it is termed, is being improperly used, there is an uneasiness in many minds about its wide scope. The House of Commons is quite conscious of the danger; in 1944 it set up a scrutinising committee to study all such orders and regulations so that any undesirable features may be brought to the attention of the House: most orders and regulations have to "lie on the table" for forty days before coming into operation; this gives an opportunity for those interested to study them and, if they so desire, criticise them. There is one judicial check; a court may rule that an order is *ultra vires*, or goes beyond the powers given in the Act.

Before we go on to describe the system of courts, something must be said about the judiciary itself.

## iii. *The Judiciary*

At the head of all is the Lord High Chancellor; we have already noted his position as a Minister and as Speaker of the House of Lords. There are two other Ministers of legal rank in the Government; the Attorney-General and the Solicitor-General; they are the legal advisers of the Government. These three Ministers may seem to contradict the statement that the law and politics are kept separate; but they are fortified by that tradition of independence that prevents them from acting in a partisan spirit in a matter of law.

The Master of the Rolls is President of the Court of Appeal. His title takes us back to the Middle Ages when his predecessors were keepers of the administrative records (a 'roll' was a length of parchment rolled up for convenience of handling). He is still responsible for the safe-keeping of all Crown Records which are now at the Public Record Office. The judges who sit in the Court of Appeal are known as Lords Justices of Appeal.

The Lord Chief Justice is the head of the High Court. While all the other judges are appointed by the King on the advice of the Lord Chancellor, the L.C.J. is appointed on the advice of the Prime Minister. This seems to contradict the non-political character of the judiciary, but the strong tradition of this high office cancels any tendency to partisanship.

There are nine Lords of Appeal in Ordinary (to be distinguished from the Lords Justices of Appeal) who sit in the House of Lords when it acts as the highest Court of Appeal. They are life peers; that is, the titles die with them. They do not take part in the normal political work of the House of Lords, and when legal cases are being considered, it is not customary for peers without legal experience to take part. The Lords of Appeal are also members of the Judicial Committee of the Privy Council which is the supreme judicial authority of the British Commonwealth and Empire; appeals come to it from the Dominions and from Consular Courts.

The Judges of the High Court are assigned to one or other of the three Divisions to be described presently.

County Court Judges are selected from practising barristers of experience. Recorders are appointed to Borough Quarter Sessions and are usually practising barristers.

This list seems a long one but it is not complete. Of the 661,748 offences tried in all courts during 1947 no fewer than 627,474 were dealt with by lay magistrates or justices of the peace. A distinguished lawyer has written:

> Just as sediment collects at the bottom of a bottle of wine, so work is thickest at the foot of the judicial ladder, and at the foot stand 'the great unpaid', the justices of the peace. Since the days of Edward I, these justices have filled a most important place, or, rather, many most important places, in the scheme of everyday life.

Until the time of Edward III they were Conservators of the Peace, but in 1344 they were given powers to try prisoners; this was the beginning of the end of the judicial work of sheriffs. More and more work, administrative as well as judicial, was added to the duties of these lay magistrates. Much of the administrative work was transferred to the County

Councils in 1888, but since then the judicial work of the justices of the peace has considerably increased. They are appointed by the Lord Chancellor on the recommendation of the Lord Lieutenant of a County who is advised by a Committee. There were about 17,000 active J.P.s in England and Wales in 1948, nearly 4000 being women.

Most J.P.s have had no legal experience before appointment, and it is sometimes asked if this system of laymen giving judgment and sentence is the best that could be devised. There is no similar scheme in any other country. A Royal Commission on Justices of the Peace was appointed in 1946 to study the subject. With one exception the members of that Commission recommended that the present system should be retained but with some improvements in the method of appointment and retirement. One passage from the report in support of the existing system may be quoted.

> Lawyers themselves would be the last to claim that legal training by itself is a sufficient equipment for one called upon to give decisions on questions of fact where reputation and liberty are at stake.... The present system is to be commended because, like that of trial by jury, it gives the citizen a part to play in the administration of the law. It emphasises the fact that the principles of the common law, and even the language of statutes, ought to be comprehensible by any intelligent person without specialised training. Its continuance prevents the growth of a suspicion in the ordinary man's mind that the law is a mystery which must be left to a professional caste and has little in common with justice as the layman understands it.

The functions of J.P.s are sometimes misunderstood. A bench of magistrates is really like a jury and the first duty is to decide on the facts according to the evidence; if the verdict is 'Guilty', then they proceed to settle the penalty. They are guided as to the law by their Clerk who is a trained lawyer. It should also be remembered that the convicted person has the right of appeal to a higher court.

Some towns have Stipendiary Magistrates, that is lawyers who are paid salaries; but the power to make such appointments is not widely used, and in 1948 there were only sixteen such magistrates. In London there are twenty-six Metropolitan Police Magistrates who are Stipendiaries.

## iv. *The Courts of Law*

We must now review the system of courts; the table on p. 157 will be a guide. The whole is divided vertically into two parts; the left is labelled 'Criminal' and the right 'Civil'. Criminal Law deals with offences against the community (though primarily against an individual) such as theft, assault, dangerous driving and so on. The Crown prosecutes; that is why cases are referred to as *Rex* v. *So-and-so*. Civil Law concerns relations between private individuals or companies or corporations. Breach of contract and the interpretation of wills are examples.

At the bottom of the table is the heading 'Courts of Summary Jurisdiction'; 'summary' here means 'immediate' or 'speedy'. We usually call these courts Petty Sessions, Police Courts, or Magistrates' Courts. They have very little to do with civil cases though they can deal with a few types of matrimonial cases, claims for wages, rates and rents.

Most civil cases begin in one of the 450 County Courts; these are not strictly arranged according to Counties; they are grouped in eight circuits each of which is toured by a judge.

More serious civil cases may go to the High Court. This is in three Divisions.

1. *King's Bench Division*. This deals with most civil cases—breaches of contract, insurance, income tax, etc.

2. *Chancery Division*. This deals with cases affecting estates, mortgages, trusts, etc.

3. *Probate, Divorce and Admiralty*. Cases of probate (wills) and divorce used to come under the Ecclesiastical Courts; the Admiralty section deals with collisions, etc. The work of the divorce section has become so congested in

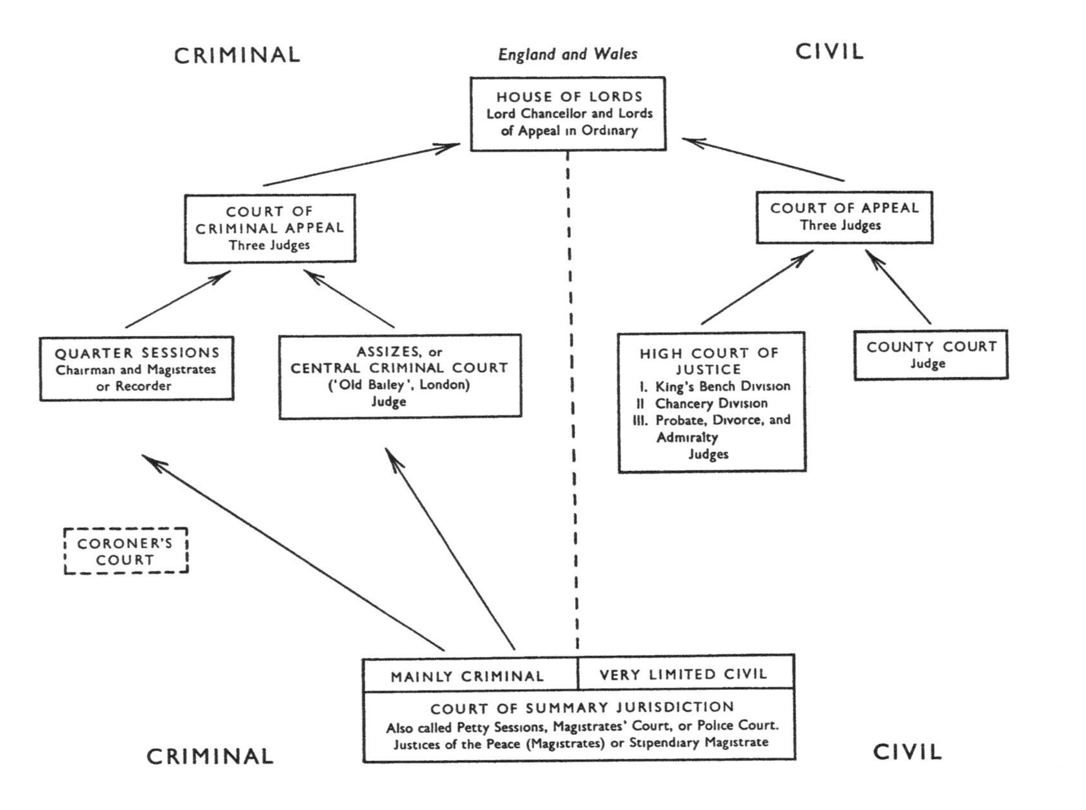
CRIMINAL
England and Wales
CIVIL
HOUSE OF LORDS
Lord Chancellor and Lords of Appeal in Ordinary
COURT OF CRIMINAL APPEAL
Three Judges
COURT OF APPEAL
Three Judges
QUARTER SESSIONS
Chairman and Magistrates or Recorder
ASSIZES, or CENTRAL CRIMINAL COURT
('Old Bailey', London)
Judge
HIGH COURT OF JUSTICE
I. King's Bench Division
II Chancery Division
III. Probate, Divorce, and Admiralty
Judges
COUNTY COURT
Judge
CORONER'S COURT
MAINLY CRIMINAL
VERY LIMITED CIVIL
COURT OF SUMMARY JURISDICTION
Also called Petty Sessions, Magistrates' Court, or Police Court.
Justices of the Peace (Magistrates) or Stipendiary Magistrate
CRIMINAL
CIVIL

recent years that County Court Judges now also act as Commissioners for matrimonial cases.

Above the High Court of Justice and County Courts comes the Court of Appeal. It has already been mentioned that the right of appeal from one court to a higher is a principle of our system of justice. This is seldom done for frivolous reasons; one salutary check is that sentences may be increased as well as decreased or quashed.

Let us return to the bottom of the table and work up the left-hand side, the criminal law.

We have seen how great a proportion of cases are dealt with in Magistrates' Courts. Even in the most serious cases, such as murder, the first hearing is held in one of these Courts; this is not a trial but an examination to ensure that there is sufficient evidence to justify the case going to a higher court. For the more serious offences the accused has the right to be tried before a jury at a higher court; but he may, in some cases, be tried summarily if he so wishes. Many prefer to do so, especially if they know the evidence against them is conclusive; they also save much time by being tried at Petty Sessions. Juvenile Courts are also held by magistrates; more must be said of these later in this chapter.

Quarter Sessions are held in every county four times a year. The court consists of county magistrates with a chairman who is usually an experienced barrister; in some cities and boroughs a Recorder sits alone.

Assizes are held in county towns three or four times a year for the trial of the most serious offences, though less serious cases may be taken if the date of Assizes comes earlier than that of Quarter Sessions; this is to bring speedy justice and so avoid keeping the accused in prison or on bail for too long a period. Bail means that an accused person is released until his trial on undertaking to appear in court and giving satisfactory sureties. Bail is not allowed for the most serious crimes or if there is any suspicion that the accused may abscond. The ceremony with which Assizes open on the arrival of the

High Court Judge in a town is a relic of history and serves to emphasise the seriousness of the occasion.

The Assizes in London are at 'Old Bailey', the Central Criminal Court; cases of grave character are taken there from the provinces if this is felt desirable. Local excitement may make it difficult to conduct the case calmly or for the members of the jury to keep unbiased.

The Court of Criminal Appeal is in London; three judges of the High Court take the cases.

For both civil and criminal cases, the House of Lords is the court of final appeal; for an appeal to be heard it is necessary to have the consent of the Attorney-General to ensure that the case is sufficiently serious.

Reference must be made to one court that lies outside the main system. The Coroner's Court is almost entirely concerned with unexplained deaths; the Coroner (appointed by the County or County Borough Council) holds an inquest with a jury to investigate the circumstances of a suspicious death provided the body is available. This is not in any sense a trial, though the verdict may be the prelude to police action. The office of Coroner is an ancient one going back to the twelfth century, but most of his former duties have been transferred. In addition to 'sitting on the body' the Coroner holds inquests on treasure trove. He no longer holds inquests on wrecks, or on 'royal fish'—that is, whales or sturgeon that may be washed ashore or caught.

The legal profession is divided into two parts—solicitors and barristers. The term 'attorney' as alternative to barrister was abolished in 1873 and only survives in the title of the Attorney-General. Anyone wanting advice on the law goes to a solicitor; he is allowed to plead for a client in Petty Sessions or in the County Court. In all the higher courts only a barrister is allowed to plead, and his services are secured by a solicitor, not by the client. Barristers may become judges or be appointed to other high legal office.

The Law Society lays down the qualifications for the

admission of solicitors; a candidate serves articles as a clerk in a solicitor's office and has to pass certain examinations. After being admitted by the Master of the Rolls, a solicitor may go into private practice, or seek such a public appointment as Town Clerk, or Clerk of the Peace, or an appointment with a commercial company.

Barristers belong to one or other of the four ancient Inns of Court—Gray's Inn, Lincoln's Inn, the Inner Temple, or the Middle Temple. To qualify a candidate has to keep twelve terms at his Inn, and if he then satisfies by examination the requirements laid down by the Benchers of his Inn, he is 'called to the Bar', and can practise in the courts; but he may have to wait some time before he gets his first 'brief'—that is, receives instructions from a solicitor to plead in a case. After practising ten years as a Junior Counsel wearing a plain stuff gown, he may apply to the Lord Chancellor to become a King's Counsel (K.C.), or 'take silk', that is, wear a silk gown. A K.C. is, by etiquette, debarred from taking certain types of minor business, but for an able man the change of status is an opportunity for highest achievement.

## v. *Prisons and Borstals*

It is not necessary here to relate the history of prisons; it contains some dreadful pages recording brutalities and cruelties that to us would seem incredible were it not that even greater (because more refined) cruelties have been committed in this century in countries where the State is all and the individual nothing.

Old ideas die hard and it has taken the devoted work of men and women of a century or more to bring about the revolution that has taken place in our treatment of prisoners. The dominant motives used to be retribution and intimidation. Now it is true that the community must be protected from lawless men and women and there is undoubtedly a small but dangerous criminal class against whom it is necessary to take the strictest action. But this does not mean that the majority of those convicted in our courts are beyond redemption. The new ideas were well put by the Prison Commissioners in their report for 1923.

> Since an offender has to return to ordinary life and take his place as a citizen and earn his living at some time in the future, which is usually not far distant, our object is to fit him for those duties. The means to this end are fairly long hours of hard and steady work at an occupation which shall, if possible, give such industrial training as will enable him to earn a living, the removal of needless degradations and the encouragement of self-respect: and in the evenings, well-considered education suitable for backward or unbalanced adults. To these are added visiting from voluntary workers of strong character and personal influence, and, where possible, such measure of trust as will awaken a sense of personal responsibility.

An important step forward was taken when it was decided to classify prisoners rather carefully. Those whose records suggest the best hope of a steady future are put in the Star class and are allowed some responsibility and privileges; the Ordinary class consists of those whose previous records or the nature of their offences suggest the need for strict discipline; there is always the possibility of promotion to the Star class; the Convict class consists of long-sentence prisoners with bad records; they are sent to special prisons such as Dartmoor which is used for the worst recidivists (habitual criminals). The old terms 'penal servitude' and 'hard labour' are no longer used; it is felt better for the exact character of the discipline and treatment to be left to those who are in close association with the prisons.

One purpose of this system is to prevent 'old lags' having a bad influence on those who have a chance of putting themselves right with society on leaving prison. This danger is particularly serious for young men and women. The aim now is to avoid sending anyone under twenty-one to one of the usual prisons.

An alternative to prison was tried out at Borstal, a village near Rochester, in 1902; the young men were given a larger measure of movement and association than is usual in a prison. The success of the experiment has led to an extension of the system. There are now seven Borstal Institutions for young men and one for young women aged between sixteen and twenty-one on the day of conviction.

## vi. *Juveniles*

Under the Children Act of 1908 trials of young offenders (under seventeen) must be held in special rooms and not in the usual Police Courts. Some towns have built, or have planned to build, separate Juvenile Courts. This step was taken because it was realised that harm was done to these juveniles by bringing them into contact with ordinary courts and sometimes with adult prisoners. An Act of 1933 further developed this idea. It was felt desirable to make the proceedings as informal as possible and to create a kindly atmosphere. The public is not admitted, but newspaper representatives are allowed to make reports provided they do not give names or pictures.

Great care is taken to find out the home circumstances of the child and any other influences that may have encouraged the offence. This kind of inquiry is carried out by Probation Officers who do admirable work in helping to keep youngsters straight. Very often the child is put under the supervision of one of these officers, and the friendliness that develops is an important factor in the child's life and conduct.

More serious cases may lead to committal to an Approved School (such a school used to be called a Reformatory). These are well-run institutions where the youngster can grow up in healthy surroundings with every encouragement to develop his abilities. Much has still to be done in this kind of special training but the right direction has been taken.

CHAPTER XVIII

# HOW WE CAN HELP

Whether we are electors or not yet electors we can all help the community by keeping ourselves informed about current affairs. By our home surroundings and other conditions, each of us is predisposed towards one or other of the political Parties. It is not an easy matter to take an objective view of public questions; we speak of the 'open mind' but that is just as likely to be the 'vacant mind'; what we need to do is to make a habit of getting as complete a presentation of facts as possible and then studying them in relation to the declared policies of the parties. This is where group or team study has an advantage over private study, provided that the group is not formed on a party basis. The clash of opinions is a valuable means of clarifying our own views.

The newspaper and the broadcast news bulletins are the most obvious sources of information.

Our newspapers are free from Government control or censorship. Each has its political outlook though this is not always a strictly party point of view. We do, to some extent, suffer from the fact that so many of the newspapers are controlled by a few commercial groups; this inevitably means a restriction in the variety of opinions expressed. It is natural that a newspaper should put emphasis on news that supports its own policy; this does not mean deliberate falsification, but there are many ways of presenting news; the use of large-type headlines, the position in which the news is placed, as well as the amount of space given to any item, are all means to impress upon readers the importance given by the newspaper to parts of the news.

It has sometimes been suggested that a newspaper is needed giving plain accounts of events or summaries of speeches without comment. Such a product would be very dull reading. There is evidence, for example in election results, that newspapers have less effect on public opinion than they claim to have.

The bulletins broadcast by the B.B.C. do not set out to express a point of view; their aim is to give the news as plainly as possible within the time available. A report on Parliament is broadcast at a late hour.

Both the newspapers and the B.B.C. get much of their information from agencies such as Reuters in addition to receiving reports from 'our own correspondent'. Reuters was the first and most famous of the agencies. It was begun in 1849 by Paul Reuter in Aachen; he used pigeons as well as the telegraph; his business was transferred to London in 1851. An interesting book on this subject is *From Pigeon Post to Wireless* by H. M. Collins.

Neither the newspapers nor the B.B.C. can give anything like a full report of Parliamentary proceedings. Some papers pick out 'incidents' for special prominence. If one Honourable Member punches another on the nose, it is NEWS, but a well-argued speech is not news. For full reports we must go to Hansard; two daily reports are issued, one for the House of Lords and the other for the Commons. A weekly edition of the Commons debates is also published. These reports should be available in every public library.

For a long time Parliament refused to allow its debates to be reported. Various subterfuges were adopted to get round the prohibition. From 1740 to 1743 Dr Johnson wrote reports for *The Gentleman's Magazine*; these were based on scanty notes supplied by an attender in the public gallery, but Johnson so wrote these up that he made every speaker use his own sonorous style but taking "care that the Whig dogs should not have the best of it". Under pressure of public opinion the Commons relaxed their ruling to the extent of allowing reporters to make shorthand records, but no facilities were offered for their accommodation. It was not until 1834 that a special gallery was set aside for them. Perhaps the most famous of such reporters was Charles Dickens who began in 1832; his reports were noted for their accuracy. William Cobbett (1762–1835) published reports in the early years of the nineteenth century; from 1808 these were printed by T. C. Hansard. Later the Treasury made small grants towards the continuation of these reports, but it was not until 1909 that the House took over full responsibility and engaged a staff of reporters. The Hansard family has long ceased to have any connection with the reports but in 1944 the name was restored to the title-page which reads

PARLIAMENTARY DEBATES
(Hansard)

It is essential that anyone desiring to get a true notion of public affairs should read Hansard. The reading of even an occasional issue will show that the House of Commons is a very live assembly; the debates are serious discussions of principles and of the detailed applications of policy. Of course there are repetitions of argument and some speakers are long-winded; but that is usual in any gathering of debaters.

Some readers may wish to follow up particular aspects of the subjects treated in these pages. A few books may be suggested for the next stage of study.

### THE CONSTITUTION

Walter Bagehot's *The English Constitution*, in spite of having been written as long ago as 1867, is still valuable; it should be read in the World's Classics edition as this has an introduction by Earl Balfour based on his long experience of public affairs.

*The British Constitution* by W. Ivor Jennings (Cambridge University Press, 1941) is a stimulating book. This could be followed by the same author's larger books, *Cabinet Government* (1936), and *Parliament* (1939), from the same publishers.

On the historical side S. B. Chrimes's *English Constitutional History* (Home University Library, Oxford University Press, 1947) is a good introduction and has a useful bibliography.

PARLIAMENT

For the actual working of Parliament the authoritative introduction is *Parliament* by Sir Courtenay Ilbert, revised by Sir Cecil Carr (3rd edition, 1948, Home University Library). A more informal book is *Our Parliament* by S. Gordon. This is published by the Hansard Society whose purpose it is to create wider interest in the reports of Parliamentary proceedings.

Between the wars a useful series of books called "The Whitehall Series" (Putnam) was published dealing with the Ministries; *Home Office*, *Ministry of Health*, *Treasury*, etc. Although there have since been changes in the functions of some of the Ministries, these books are not out of date; each contains an account of the history of the Ministry. A similar book is *G.P.O.* by E. T. Crutchley (Cambridge University Press).

His Majesty's Stationery Office (H.M.S.O.) publishes many informative and inexpensive pamphlets and booklets; for instance, the Careers Series contains pamphlets on the Civil Service, the Local Government Service, the Police, the Probation Officer, etc. The publications of H.M.S.O. are not too well known, and those living in one of the large towns where there is a sales office, should go along to see what is available. Others should write to ask if anything is published on any aspect of public affairs in which they are interested; they will be surprised to find how wide is the scope of this national service.

H.M.S.O. publishes all official reports and statements of policy. The bulkier ones are usually bound in blue paper covers and so are known as Blue Books; smaller reports are called White Papers as they have no cover.

For statistics the most useful publication is the *Annual*

*Abstract of Statistics* (H.M.S.O.) Another handy source of information is *Whitaker's Almanack*.

THE LAW

Geldart's *Elements of English Law* revised by Sir William Holdsworth and H. G. Hanbury (Home University Library) is a good introduction. *Common Sense in Law*, by Sir Paul Vinogradoff and H. G. Hanbury (Home University Library) should be read. H. G. Hanbury's *English Courts of Law* in the same series is not easy reading; it deals with the subject historically and the material does not allow popular treatment; the book will repay careful study. *The Book of English Law* by E. Jenks (Murray) was written for laymen and is very readable. *Outlines of Criminal Law* by C. S. Kenny and *The Machinery of Justice in England* by R. M. Jackson (both published by the Cambridge University Press) are standard books.

*Crime and the Community* by Sir Leo Page (Faber) discusses many important problems and is written for the layman. The best book on Juvenile Courts is *The Child and the Magistrate* by J. A. F. Watson (Cape).

Two booklets published by H.M.S.O. are worth getting: *Prisons and Borstals*, and *Making Citizens* (Approved Schools).

It is hoped that the reader has already noted a number of problems for further consideration. Here are a few for him to think over:

1. What are the differences between the powers of our King and those of the President of the U.S.A.?

2. Do you think a Second Chamber is desirable? If so, suggest a constitution for one.

3. Is a member of Parliament a delegate or a representative?

4. Do you think that the broadcasting of debates from the House of Commons is desirable?

5. In *The English Constitution* Bagehot wrote in 1867, "So well is our Government concealed that if you tell a cabman to drive to Downing Street he will most likely never have heard of it". This is certainly not true of the present-day taxi-driver. To what do you attribute the change?

6. How far does the daily newspaper influence the political opinions of people you meet?

7. Can you suggest ways in which broadcasting could do more to keep people informed of public questions?

8. What are the dangers of justice being administered by a lay and untrained body of magistrates? What improvements would you suggest? (A visit to Petty Sessions should be made before thinking out this question.)

9. Do you think that our prisons are getting too 'soft'?

10. Do you think that Scotland and Wales should have their own Parliaments as Northern Ireland has?

## Here are some suggestions for Groups or Teams.

1. Invite such experts as the following to meet your Group: a Probation Officer, a J.P., a Civil Servant. Prepare beforehand a list of well thought-out questions to put to your visitor.

2. Compare the report in one issue of Hansard (Commons) with the reports in several daily newspapers. Each member of the Group should have a different paper.

3. Organise a mimic Parliament; if your Group is too small, invite the co-operation of Youth Organisations.

4. Collect figures for the last two Parliamentary elections in your local constituency. Are you satisfied that minority views get fair play?

5. Study the Budget figures for the current year.

6. Organise (*a*) a mimic sitting of Petty Sessions, and (*b*) a mimic sitting of a Juvenile Court.

7. Debate the following comment on the Party system by Mr George Bernard Shaw.

> "The effect of this system is that measures brought before the House by the Government are never voted on their merits but solely on the question whether the Government shall remain in office or not, and whether all the members of the House shall be put to the expense and trouble of an immediate election at which their seats will be at stake."

8. Make up ten questions you would like to ask Ministers in the House of Commons.

9. Should candidates for Parliament be obliged to pass a test of competence? Devise such a test.

10. In what ways can public opinion influence Parliament?

# THE BRITISH COMMUNITY

## CHAPTER XIX

## EMPIRE AND COMMONWEALTH

We are shy of using the word 'Empire' when we speak of the British Community, but there is no need to be apologetic even if some now use 'Imperialist' as a term of abuse. Our present has grown out of our past, and however much we may regret the lawless actions of some unscrupulous men we have more reason to be proud of the great achievements of men of fine ideals who made possible our present association of peace-loving communities united by common purposes and traditions.

A Committee of the Imperial Conference that met in 1926 issued a report from which the following extracts are taken. They deserve most careful reading.

> The Committee are of opinion that nothing would be gained by attempting to lay down a Constitution for the British Empire. Its widely scattered parts have very different characteristics, very different histories, and are at very different stages of evolution; while, considered as a whole, it defies classification and bears no resemblance to any other political organisation which now exists or has ever yet been tried.
>
> There is, however, one most important element in it which, from a strictly constitutional point of view, has now, as regards all vital matters, reached its full development—we refer to the group of self-governing communities composed of Great Britain and the Dominions. Their position and mutual relation may be readily defined. *They are autonomous Communities within the British Empire, equal in status, in no way subordinate one to another in any aspect of their domestic or external affairs, though united by a common allegiance to the Crown, and freely associated as members of the British Commonwealth of Nations....*
>
> The rapid evolution of the Oversea Dominions during the last fifty years has involved many complicated adjustments of old political machinery to changing conditions. The tendency towards equality of status was both right and inevitable. Geographical and other conditions made this impossible of attainment by the way of federation. The only alternative was by the way of autonomy; and along this road it has been steadily

sought. Every self-governing member of the Empire is now the master of its own destiny. In fact, if not always in form, it is subject to no compulsion whatever.

But no account, however accurate, of the negative relations in which Great Britain and the Dominions stand to each other can do more than express a portion of the truth. The British Empire is not founded upon negations. It depends essentially, if not formally, on positive ideals. Free institutions are its life-blood. Free co-operation is its instrument. Peace, security, and progress are among its objects.

Four phrases in the first of the quoted paragraphs call for comment.

(1) ...*different characteristics*....

This was the most obvious fact about the Empire in 1926 and subsequent developments have not greatly changed the general picture. Its members were to be found in all continents and oceans; every variety of climate and of wild life and vegetation was known somewhere in the Empire. Of its more than five hundred million inhabitants only seventy million were white; the rest included people of innumerable races. Only a minority of its peoples were Christian. Within the Empire the whole range of culture from the most primitive to the most civilised could be studied.

(2) ...*very different histories*....

It is not possible here even to summarise the history of the Empire, but a few points of general application may be noted. No statesman or group of statesmen planned the extension of the Empire. There is some truth in the statement made by Sir John Seeley that "we seem to have conquered and peopled half the world in a fit of absence of mind". Far from scheming this extension leading statesmen of last century up to about 1875 regarded the colonies as a burden; even Disraeli could say in 1852 "these wretched colonies...are a millstone round our necks". The last quarter of the nineteenth century saw a change of attitude and it was then that enthusiasm for the

Empire swelled to considerable, and sometimes blatant, dimensions. But this Imperialist phase died down after the Boer War.

We may note five ways in which the Empire was extended; two or more of these might be concurrent.

(i) The spirit of adventure and the love of exploration took our forefathers to all parts of the world. These were the pioneers who rarely gained any material advantage from their discoveries.

(ii) Others were traders seeking for new markets or to bring to the home market the luxuries and products of distant lands. In this the Chartered Companies, such as the Hudson's Bay Company, played a leading part. Trading posts or ports were established and this inevitably led to relations with the inhabitants. Sometimes there was what is called 'exploitation', but the basis was the natural desire of a merchant to extend his business. The East India Company is the outstanding example of this process; as Burke said, "The constitution of the Company began in commerce and ended in empire". Let us not be too ready to see any deeply-laid scheme in all this; there were, as always, unprincipled men, but there were also many honest men—otherwise the British would never have gained the high reputation they did gain.

(iii) Some colonies were gained by conquest; Canada is the outstanding example, though it should be noted that the main purpose of the war was not the acquisition of that country from the French.

(iv) Other lands were added by settlement; this was possible where the indigenous population, as in North America or Australia, was too small to occupy the territory effectively. People went from various motives; some were escaping from religious or political persecution; others were in search of new land that they could own and develop; others were acting from a spirit of adventure; some were sent against their will as a penalty for rebellion or crime; others were fugitives from justice or their creditors.

(v) The desire to spread Christianity has taken many fine men and women to far distant places where they have carried on their missions in spite of dangers and fierce opposition—often at the cost of their lives. Supercilious critics have sneered at the missionaries and have said that they pioneered the way for the trader and the flag. Missionaries—like other men—have made their mistakes, but these are outweighed a thousand times by the good they have done; they have turned people from cruel superstitions and have shown them a better way of life; they have been the pioneers of schools and of hospitals—work that was not undertaken by the Government till a much later period.

(3) ...*different stages of evolution*....

Evolution to what? For many to a more peaceful and secure life; at times (and in some places to-day) it has also meant a kind of industrial bondship that is little better than slavery. For all parts of the Empire the evolution has been towards an increasing measure of self-government until full national sovereignty is achieved. That this is no idle theory is demonstrated by the histories of the Dominions, of Southern Ireland and of India and Burma. The rate of progress depends on the degree of education and capacity for responsibility in each colony.

(4) ...*it defies classification*....

The truth of this will soon become apparent if the reader will attempt to group the members of the Commonwealth under headings according to the stage of self-government each has attained; any scheme soon breaks down; no two colonies, for instance, have exactly the same form of government; they are not forced into a few moulds since each is a separate problem.

Perhaps the most striking illustration of this characteristic is that no single label can satisfactorily be applied to this community of peoples. British Empire? Commonwealth? Or what? Speaking in the House of Commons on 2 May 1949, the Prime Minister said:

> Terminology, if it is to be useful, keeps step with developments without becoming rigid or doctrinaire. All constitutional developments in the Commonwealth, the British Commonwealth, or the British Empire—I use the three terms deliberately—have been the subject of consultation between His Majesty's Governments, and there has been no agreement to adopt or to exclude the use of any one of these terms, nor any decision on the part of His Majesty's Government in the United Kingdom to do so... I think it better to allow people to use the expression they like best.

In April 1949 there was a meeting of the Prime Ministers of 'His Majesty's Governments' to consider the position of India. That country had expressed its intention of becoming an independent republic, but, at the same time, desired to be associated with the Commonwealth. How could this be done? As a result of the discussions, the following statement was made in the House of Commons on 28 April:

> The Government of India have informed the other Governments of the Commonwealth of the intention of the Indian people that under the new constitution which is about to be adopted India shall become a sovereign independent republic. The Government of India have however declared and affirmed India's desire to continue her full membership of the Commonwealth of Nations and her acceptance of the King as the symbol of the free association of its independent member nations and as such the Head of the Commonwealth.
>
> The Governments of the other countries of the Commonwealth, the basis of whose membership of the Commonwealth is not hereby changed, accept and recognise India's continuing membership in accordance with the terms of this declaration.
>
> Accordingly the United Kingdom, Canada, Australia, New Zealand, South Africa, India, Pakistan and Ceylon hereby declare that they remain united as free and equal members of the Commonwealth of Nations, freely co-operating in the pursuit of peace, liberty, and progress.

Such a statement is the despair of the strict logician for it seems to reconcile contradictory ideas. But an even more difficult problem has had to be faced. By the British Nationality Act, 1948, it was enacted that citizenship of a Commonwealth country should be the qualification for being a British subject —thus reversing previous practice; the Eire Government did not agree with this, so the Act provided that Eire citizens in the United Kingdom should be treated as British subjects, and any who so wished could become citizens of 'the United Kingdom and Colonies' (not, be it noted, of the British Commonwealth and Empire). The situation again changed when Eire declared itself to be the Republic of Ireland and left the British Commonwealth. So the Ireland Act, 1949, was passed at Westminster. This recognised the Republic but declared that it is not a foreign country. A passage from the Prime Minister's speech on the Second Reading summed up the position:

> As everybody knows, there are in Britain large numbers of people of Irish descent, some born in Eire and some born in this country, and there is a continual passage to and fro of people who come over to work or to study or for pleasure. It would be an extremely difficult thing to decide in every case from day to day as to what the exact status was of a person with an Irish name, and if we had had to attempt to make all citizens of Eire aliens, it would have involved a great expenditure of men and money and a great extension of the control of aliens. We had in particular also to remember the difficulties caused because of the fact of the land frontier between Northern Ireland, which is part of the United Kingdom and the Commonwealth, and Eire.
>
> We therefore came to the conclusion that we should reciprocally decide that the people of Eire and the people of Britain should not be foreign to one another. Indeed, I go further. The same action may be taken by other Commonwealth countries. I do not pretend that the solution at which we arrived is completely logical—very few things in the relationship between these islands have been completely logical—but I believe they are practical and I believe that they are to our mutual benefit. I am aware, of course, that hitherto there has been this division in international law—it has come down from the past—in which one has recognised people as either belonging or foreign, but international law is made for men, not men for

international law. We are moving into a time when various other relationships are being created. Therefore we thought this was the most practical solution.

If that passage is carefully considered it will be found to contain evidence of that practical political wisdom that has maintained, and can continue to maintain, the links between countries of widely varying characteristics.

In the next two chapters we must consider in greater detail some of these variations both in the Dominions and in the Colonies.

CHAPTER XX

# DOMINION STATUS

It will help us to get a clearer picture of the Dominions if we briefly note some facts about the four which have the longest experience—Canada, Australia, New Zealand, and the Union of South Africa.

## i. *Canada*

The form of government in Canada is federal: that is to say, each province has its own local Legislature and controls its own internal affairs. This form of government is almost inevitable in a country which has been settled by different communities. Each had become almost a State of its own, and tended to regard its neighbours with suspicion. This made it difficult to have a unitary system of government, but by each State looking after itself and sending its representatives to a central Parliament, it has proved possible to break down the barriers between province and province, and so form a federation of States. The Dominion Parliament of Canada at Ottawa consists of an Upper House, or Senate, of ninety-six members nominated by the Governor-General in Council. The Executive Council, or Cabinet, consists of the heads of the various departments. The House of Commons consists of 255 members elected by the Provinces. A new Parliament has to be called every five years unless dissolved previously. Each Province has its own Lieutenant-Governor appointed by the Dominion Government.

A determining factor in Canadian history is the presence of a large population of French extraction. Readers of Gilbert Parker's romances will be familiar with this fact and will also have gained some idea of the earlier stages of Canada's history.

The best picture of French-Canadian life is given in *Maria Chapdelaine* by Louis Hemon.

The country was first settled by the French under Jacques Cartier in 1534; another Frenchman, Samuel Champlain, founded Quebec in 1608. It was not until 1763 that the country was ceded to Great Britain. Since that time there has been a strong French-speaking element. The Quebec Act of 1774 gave the French Canadians the use of their language and religion (Roman Catholic) and equal status with other settlers; for a period there were two Canadas, Upper and Lower, corresponding to Ontario and Quebec; but this meant constant friction. Upper Canada was occupied largely by loyalists who left the United States when the Declaration of Independence was made. Lord Durham was sent out in 1838 as Governor-General to try to heal the differences between the two Canadas. His report urged that Canada should enjoy full autonomy in its internal affairs, but the attempt at union was a failure. The Canadians themselves worked out a plan for federation, and this was established by the British North America Act of 1867, and the Dominion of Canada came into being on 1 July of that year (Dominion Day).

Canada on the south has a frontier of about 3000 miles. For much of that distance it is not a natural geographical boundary, but a line of latitude. It is a striking fact that without a large standing army, or an elaborate system of defence, peace has been preserved with her neighbour, the United States; occasional disputes have been inevitable, but these have been settled amicably.

Experience gained in Canada has determined to a great extent the development of the other Dominions.

The Provinces (and capitals) are:

Alberta (Edmonton)
British Columbia (Victoria)
Manitoba (Winnipeg)

New Brunswick (Fredericton)
Nova Scotia (Halifax)
Ontario (Toronto)
Prince Edward Island (Charlottetown)
Quebec (Quebec)
Saskatchewan (Regina)
Yukon Territory (Dawson)
North West Territories (administered from
Ottawa, which is also the federal capital)
Newfoundland & Labrador (St John's)

The total population in 1946 was estimated at 12,307,000, of whom just over half live in the provinces of Ontario and Quebec. The leading races are: British—nearly six millions; other European—five and a half million, of whom three and a half million are French-Canadians. The Red Indians number 118,316 and are declining; there are also over seven thousand Eskimos whose numbers are increasing.
The chief religions are:

| | |
|---|---|
| Roman Catholic | 4,986,552 |
| United Church of Canada | 2,204,875 |
| Anglican | 1,751,188 |

## ii. *Australia*

Australia has been occupied by settlement. Dutch explorers during the seventeenth century sailed along the coast, but it was Captain Cook in the eighteenth century who first drew attention to the island. Sydney in New South Wales (the original colony) was settled in 1788 as a convict establishment under Governor Philip. The Gold Rush of the fifties of last century meant a large increase in the population and stressed the need for establishing a settled form of government. New South Wales, Victoria, South Australia, Tasmania had each achieved responsible government by 1855. Queensland became a separate State in 1859. The need for some kind of central government gradually asserted itself and on 1 January 1901 the Commonwealth of Australia was established. Here as in Canada the form is federal, with the Commonwealth capital at Canberra. The central Government consists of a Senate of thirty-six, elected by the States, and a House of Representatives numbering seventy-five. A Federal High Court has been established to decide matters of dispute between the central Government and the individual States. A Governor is appointed by the Crown to each State, where there is a legislature of two Houses; each State is self-governing except in matters reserved to the central Government.

The States (and capitals) are:

New South Wales (Sydney)
Queensland (Brisbane)
South Australia (Adelaide)
Tasmania (Hobart)
Victoria (Melbourne)
Western Australia (Perth)

Canberra, the Australian Commonwealth capital, situated about 200 miles south-west of Sydney, is in the Capital Territory of nearly a thousand square miles. The Northern Territory of over half a million square miles is administered from Darwin by the Commonwealth. It is very sparsely inhabited owing to the nature of the country.

Of the total population of seven and a half millions, more than six and a half millions are of European extraction. Australia follows a policy of a 'White Australia' though it well understands that with such great areas to be developed it must increase rapidly and substantially the immigration of white settlers. The overcrowded lands of the Far East are a constant challenge to the Australians if they are to avoid Asiatic immigration.

The chief religions are:

| | |
|---|---|
| Church of England | 2,565,118 |
| Roman Catholic | 1,161,455 |
| Presbyterians | 713,229 |
| Methodists | 684,022 |

## iii. *New Zealand*

New Zealand was also explored by Captain Cook during the eighteenth century, but it was not until the early part of the nineteenth that serious settlements were made. Colonisation was carried out according to a well devised scheme which was the work of Edward Gibbon Wakefield (a volume of his writings is published in Everyman's Library). Under this systematic immigration, prosperity was achieved more quickly than in other colonies. Responsible government was granted in 1854, and on 26 September 1907 the country became the Dominion of New Zealand.

The Dominion has a unitary form of government. The legislature consists of an Upper House, or Legislative Council, of thirty-four, appointed by the Governor-General in Council, and a House of Representatives of eighty, elected by universal adult suffrage.

New Zealand consists of two main islands; the North, in which the capital, Wellington, is situated, and the South, which has about half the population of the North Island. There are also a number of small islands.

The total population is about 1,800,000 of whom the majority are of European extraction; there are some 105,000 Maoris whose numbers are increasing; they enjoy equal rights with all other citizens. Just over 40 per cent of the total population belongs to the Church of England, about 25 per cent is Presbyterian and 13 per cent Roman Catholic.

## iv. *Union of South Africa*

The Government of the Union of South Africa is highly centralised, not federal as in the cases of Canada and Australia. The present constitution was established in 1909, and South Africa became a Dominion in 1910, eight years after the end of the Boer War. The seat of the government is Pretoria and of the legislature, Cape Town. The Governor-General is aided by an Executive Committee with a legislature of two Houses. The Senate consists of forty members, who must be white men, eight of whom are appointed by the Governor-General in Council, and each of the four provinces elects eight more. The House of Assembly consists of 150 elected members who must be British subjects of European descent. In addition to this National Parliament there are four Provincial Councils with very limited powers. The Governor-General in Council appoints an Administrator for each province.

The Provinces (and capitals) are:

Cape of Good Hope (Cape Town)
Natal (Pietermaritzburg)
Transvaal (Pretoria)
Orange Free State (Bloemfontein)

Statistics of races are not easily compiled owing to the preponderance of native Africans. Only one-fifth of the population is of European descent; rather more than half of these are Afrikanders—that is, of Dutch, French, or German origin—who now form a distinct nation of proud traditions with their own language, Afrikaans. Less than half of the white population is of British origin. The Kaffirs form the bulk of the native population; as a result of miscegenation there are many 'coloured' people. In Natal there is also a large Indian population descended from those brought in at the end of the last century to supply labour. This racial problem is the most difficult that South African statesmen have to face; the whites fear being swamped by the native Africans. It is important for us to understand the difficulties and to resist the temptation to offer 'simple' solutions that we should ourselves question if we lived in South Africa face to face with the practical issues.

From the above brief summaries it will be seen that by 1910 these four Dominions had gained complete autonomy in their internal affairs, but foreign relationships remained under the control of the Parliament at Westminster.

The outbreak of war in 1914 and the great part played by the Dominions in securing a successful end, created a new situation. Frequent consultation was necessary with the Dominions and this culminated in 1917 in the creation of an Imperial War Cabinet; the outstanding Dominion representatives were Sir Robert Borden (Canada), W. M. Hughes (Australia) and General J. C. Smuts (South Africa). From this it was an inevitable development that the Dominions should be represented at the Peace Conference in 1919 and that they should later sign the treaties on behalf of their own countries.

After the war it became clear that some clarification of the position would be necessary. A quotation has already been made from the Report of the 1926 Imperial Conference (see p. 169); this included a passage (italicised) defining the position of the Dominions. It will be noted that they were declared to be "in no way subordinate one to another in any aspect of their domestic or external affairs". The last two words represented a vital change in the position. Like so many of our declarations, this confirmed a situation that had already been established in practice.

## v. *The Statute of Westminster*

The next Imperial Conference, 1930, prepared the way for the Act of Parliament of 1931 known as 'The Statute of Westminster'. Some statesmen expressed doubts as to the wisdom of attempting to formularise the relations between Great Britain and the Dominions, but there were laws in existence, such as the Colonial Laws Validity Act of 1865, that might be invoked in difficult circumstances.

Two or three quotations from the Statute of Westminster are important statements that should be studied.

It is stated in the Preamble that "any alteration in the law touching the Succession to the Throne or the Royal Style and Titles shall hereafter require the assent as well of the Parliaments of all the Dominions as of the Parliament of the United Kingdom". From this it is clear that the King is King of each Dominion separately; in each he acts on the advice of his Ministers. His direct representatives such as Governors-General are appointed on the advice of the Dominion concerned, and in some instances such appointments have been held by Dominion citizens.

Two clauses should be noted:

> It is hereby declared and enacted that the Parliament of a Dominion has full power to make laws having extra-territorial operation.

> No Act of Parliament of the United Kingdom passed after the commencement of this Act shall extend, or be deemed to extend, to a Dominion, as part of the law of that Dominion, unless it is expressly declared in that Act that that Dominion has requested, and consented to, the enactment thereof.

One clause also finally buried the term 'colony' as applicable to any Dominion.

Some foreigners, and indeed some British citizens, wonder if it is really true that each Dominion is a sovereign state. Two examples of what has happened since the passing of the Statute of Westminster should dispel any doubts.

The first concerns the abdication of Edward VIII in 1936. While the crisis was under discussion the Dominion Prime Ministers were consulted and kept fully informed. Here was a situation that meant "an alteration in the law touching the Succession to the Throne". The Abdication Act was passed at

Westminster on 11 December with the full agreement of Canada, Australia and New Zealand. But South Africa acted separately by an Act passed on the previous day—a clear indication of policy; the Irish Free State also passed a separate Act on 12 December. So George VI became King of the Union of South Africa on 10 December, King of Great Britain and Northern Ireland and of Canada, Australia and New Zealand on 11 December, and King of the Irish Free State on 12 December. This series of events alone would be a conclusive proof of Dominion sovereignty, but three years later with the outbreak of war, a second proof was provided.

When the United Kingdom declared war at the beginning of September 1939, Australia and New Zealand at once concurred. A few days elapsed before the Canadian Parliament also declared war. In South Africa the Government under General Hertzog proposed neutrality but were defeated in Parliament; General Smuts then became Prime Minister and received majority support in declaring war. The position in Eire (now the Republic of Ireland) was even more decisive; the Dail (Parliament) decided to remain neutral, and throughout the war maintained that position though many of her citizens served under the Union Jack. The deprivation of air and naval bases in southern Ireland was a serious handicap to the United Kingdom, but the neutrality of Eire was respected.

If a third proof were needed of the genuine independence of members of the Commonwealth, the case of Burma could be cited. After the war Burma was asked to decide her future, and she chose to break from the Commonwealth; no hindrance was offered and Burma is no longer associated with the Commonwealth or Empire.

Towards the end of the last century there was much talk of the possibility of imperial federation with a Parliament representative of all the Dominions. Joseph Chamberlain was strongly in favour of this idea, but it was not until 1911 that the Prime Minister of New Zealand, Sir Joseph Ward, submitted a definite scheme, which was turned down by the Dominions. This does not mean a lack of consultation. Various methods are used.

We have already referred to the position of the Secretary for Commonwealth Relations (see p. 98). A High Commissioner for each Dominion is permanently in London and there is constant exchange of views going on between these representatives and the Secretary of State. It may be noted that the Dominions have representatives in other countries; for instance Canada and Australia have ambassadors in Washington —a further proof of national sovereignty. Another means of keeping in touch is by direct correspondence between the Prime Ministers. Since 1907 the Imperial Conference has been a recognised part of the machinery of consultation; it has no legislative power but its recommendations and the exchange of views promote smooth relationships. Thanks to air transport such conferences can now be held more frequently and, if necessary, at short notice. Meetings of all the Prime Ministers are now a more ready means of consultation than more formal Imperial Conferences. There are as well a number of specialised organisations that meet from time to time, such as the Imperial Economic Committee and the Committee for Imperial Defence.

The constitution of the British Commonwealth and Empire remains fluid; we may expect changes and adjustments in the future. Our relations with India and with the Republic of Ireland mark the beginning of a new phase—an association in all friendliness yet outside the circle of the Dominions. How this will work out, we cannot tell, but of one thing we can be sure: the more countries there are having such associations (however vaguely these are defined) the greater will be the world influence of this great company of peace-loving peoples. We need not worry too much about the strict letter of the law; the spirit of co-operation and the sharing of ideals are the things that matter.

## CHAPTER XXI

# COLONIAL TRUSTEESHIP

It has become customary to use the term 'Dependent Empire' to cover all those British countries that are not Dominions. Over three-quarters of these territories have come under our control within the last hundred years and most of them are in Africa; the remainder are chiefly islands, many in the West Indies, that have a much longer history as British possessions.

A common way of classifying these territories is to speak of Crown Colonies, Protectorates, and Trust Territories.

*Crown Colonies* are possessions gained by conquest, cession, or penetration. They are under the sovereignty of the Crown.

*Protectorates* are countries that technically retain their sovereignty under a native ruler but have put themselves under the protection of the British Crown; external relations are controlled by the United Kingdom, and British officials advise on internal administration.

*Trust Territories* were known formerly as League Mandated Territories. Before 1914 they were German possessions, but, instead of being annexed by the conquerors, each was placed under the care of one of the Powers and was governed on behalf of the League of Nations. Since the United Nations organisation was set up, these and other countries have become Trust Territories for which the governing power is answerable to the Trusteeship Council.

For practical purposes this classification has little significance. Legally neither the Protectorates nor the Trust Territories are British possessions, but as they are all administered by the United Kingdom, they present similar problems and are governed on the same principles. What are those principles?

TRUSTEESHIP

## i. *Principles of Government*

There is nothing startling as far as this country is concerned in the principle of trusteeship. Put shortly this means that our colonial territories are held for the benefit of the indigenous population. This view has a long history. It will be found, for instance, underlying the speeches of Edmund Burke on Indian affairs both in the House of Commons and at the trial of Warren Hastings (1788–95). His picturesque phrase, "the rice in his pot to every man in India", was but one expression of the principle of trusteeship. Then in 1824, Sir Thomas Munro, when administrator of Madras, said that we must continue to rule India until the people had become "sufficiently enlightened to frame a regular government for themselves, and to conduct and preserve it. Whenever such a time shall arrive, it will probably be best for both countries that the British control over India should be gradually withdrawn". That position was reached in 1947.

The same conception was the basis of a government statement on Kenya in 1923.

> The interests of the African natives must be paramount, and that if, and when, those interests and the interests of the immigrant races should conflict, the former must prevail....In the administration of Kenya His Majesty's Government regard themselves as exercising a trust on behalf of the African population; and they are unable to delegate or share this trust, the object of which may be defined as the protection and advancement of the native races.

Article 73 of the Charter of the United Nations (based on Article 22 of the League of Nations Covenant which itself owed much to the practice of the British Empire) sets out these principles in an amplified form. The members of the United Nations

> accept as a sacred trust the obligation to promote to the utmost...the well-being of the inhabitants of these territories, and, to this end:
>
> (*a*) to ensure, with due respect for the culture of the peoples concerned, their political, economic, social, and educational advancement, their just treatment, and their protection against abuses;

(*b*) to develop self-government, to take due account of the political aspirations of the peoples, and to assist them in the progressive development of their free political institutions, according to the particular circumstances of each territory and its peoples and their varying stages of advancement.

It would be absurd to claim that these principles have been consistently followed in our government of the colonies; the principles themselves have developed out of our experience and under the guidance of many officials inspired by high conceptions of their duties. Unfortunately, as in all human affairs, there have been other men with baser motives who have sought first their own material profit, or have acted with cruelty. We cannot ensure ourselves against lapses of this kind, but the position, quite apart from popular opinion, is very different from that of a hundred years ago. The telegraph, wireless and the aeroplane have meant that grievances can be quickly brought to notice, and officials can be kept informed of policy and given advice. To-day, if there is reason to suspect injustice or hardship, questions can be asked in the House of Commons within a few days of the occasion. It is possible for the Secretary of State or a representative to make a personal visit to any colony within a short time of any difficulty arising.

"To develop self-government" has long been the policy in the Empire. An examination of the present forms of government in the dependent territories reveals that the rate of advance towards self-government varies according to the standard of civilisation of the inhabitants. Some have not long emerged from a primitive and savage state; others have come a greater way towards a better conception of what living together in a community can mean.

At first the Governor may have sole responsibility for the administration under the Secretary of State; the next stage may be the formation of a nominated council under the Governor who has the last word; later a legislative council may be added containing a minority of elected and native representatives;

the number of elected members may be increased gradually as the sense of responsibility grows with experience; and so full representative government may be achieved. Dominion status, as in Ceylon, is the ultimate objective; but the time may come, as with Burma, when a country prefers to step right out of the circle of the Commonwealth.

This account is rather simplified as the steps towards self-government are not reproduced exactly in any one colony. In examining each country to see how it is governed, we should soon meet the system known as Indirect Rule. This was devised by Lord Lugard in Nigeria and has since been adopted in other colonies. Under this system the native rulers and councils are given considerable authority in the work of administration; the traditional tribal divisions are respected as far as practicable. In this way tribal loyalties are preserved and used to develop a sense of responsibility and a training in government. Lord Lugard also defined what he called the Dual Mandate; Great Britain, he wrote, "has her task, as trustee, on the one hand for the advancement of the subject races, and on the other hand for the development of material resources for the benefit of mankind". And, as he put it, "it is the aim of civilised administration to fulfil this dual mandate". He was not talking only of territories that are now Trust Territories (the former Mandated Territories) but of all colonies.

## ii. *The Gold Coast*

Instead of trying to survey the whole colonial Empire in a brief space, we shall derive more benefit by studying one example in more detail. The Gold Coast is a particularly useful specimen of colonial rule since it covers a Crown Colony, a Protectorate, and a Trust Territory within one region of government. The Gold Coast has a coastline of nearly 350 miles on the south of the big bulge of West Africa; north of the original colony is Ashanti; further north are the

Northern Territories, a Protectorate; on the east is the long strip of Togoland, a Trust Territory.

Portuguese traders were the first to visit the Gold Coast in the late fifteenth century; in the following century the English and the Dutch established trading forts, and in the seventeenth century the Swedes and the Danes joined the struggle. We cannot follow here the details of the competition between these countries; but by 1872 the English were left in control.

The Gold Coast occupation would probably have continued without much friction but for the presence of the Ashantis to the north. These people were pure negroes of a warlike character with an unusually efficient military organisation; they raided their neighbours and were intent on carrying on a profitable slave trade. Several times they successfully attacked the Portuguese and Dutch forts, but after being driven back by the British they made a treaty in 1817; other treaties followed in 1820 and 1832; these established a certain measure of stability. In 1821 the Crown took over the administration of the Gold Coast Colony and used the ports as naval bases for stopping the slave trade.

The subsequent fluctuations of policy illustrate how reluctant our Governments were during the first half of the nineteenth century to extend British rule. In 1828 it was decided to withdraw from the Gold Coast and ships were sent to bring away the merchants; they refused to go and the Government left them to manage alone. The merchants appointed one of themselves, George Maclean, as Governor; he proved, like so many others in our Empire history, a remarkable administrator. He raised the prestige of the British; abolished slave-trading; sat with the native chiefs in their courts and thus modified the rather harsh local laws. He even persuaded those under his influence to give up the human sacrifices that were a traditional part of the native superstitions.

In 1843 the Crown again assumed control but placed the Gold Coast under the Governor of Sierra Leone; separate

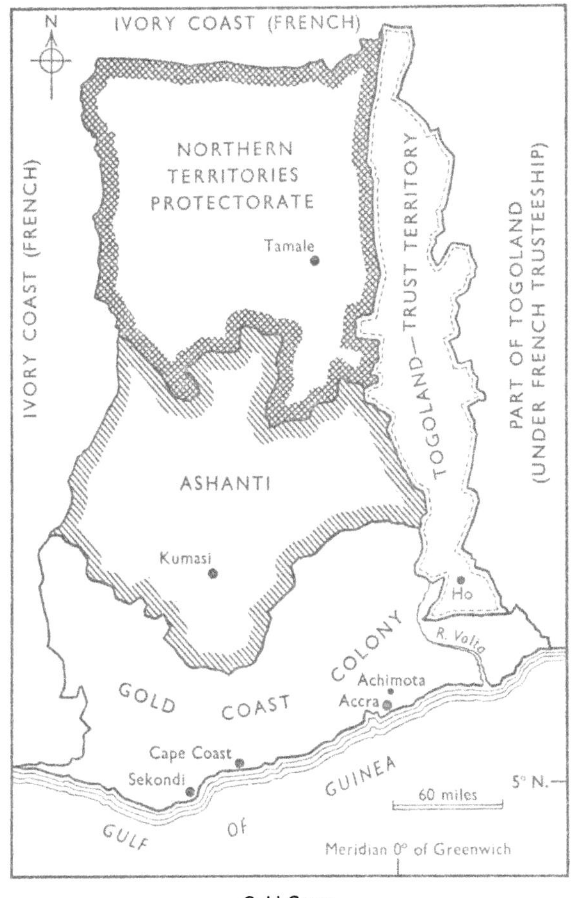
IVORY COAST (FRENCH)
N
IVORY COAST (FRENCH)
NORTHERN
TERRITORIES
PROTECTORATE
Tamale
TOGOLAND—TRUST TERRITORY
PART OF TOGOLAND
(UNDER FRENCH TRUSTEESHIP)
ASHANTI
Kumasi
Ho
R. Volta
GOLD COAST COLONY
Achimota
Accra
Cape Coast
Sekondi
GULF OF GUINEA
60 miles
5° N.
Meridian 0° of Greenwich

Gold Coast

government was granted in 1850 but in 1863, when abandonment was again contemplated, the colony was once more put under Sierra Leone. This lack of consistent policy inevitably meant a lessening of authority. Fresh Ashanti outbreaks in 1853 and 1863 seem to have influenced policy at home. Again in 1873 the Ashantis became troublesome to all their neighbours, and Sir Garnet Wolseley was sent out as Governor and Commander-in-Chief to settle the problem; he defeated the Ashantis but when they asked that their country should become a Protectorate, their request was refused. In 1886 the British offered to make the country a Protectorate, but this time the Ashantis refused! Ten years later they again began attacking surrounding tribes; an expedition was sent to Kumasi (the capital of Ashanti); there was no fighting and the King, Prempeh, was deported to the Seychelles. He was allowed to return in 1926. The sacred grove for blood-sacrifices was burnt down, and the blood-bowl was removed. (It is not without interest that the commander of the scouts on this expedition was Major R. S. S. Baden-Powell; in 1924 some of the grandsons of his native scouts were at the Boy Scout Jamboree at Wembley.) In 1901 Ashanti was annexed to the British Crown. The present Northern Territories became a Protectorate in 1897, and in 1922 Great Britain accepted the mandate for part of Togoland.

The following passage, quoted from the *Report* on the Gold Coast for 1947, well illustrates the changing attitudes of officials. In the first part we see how native traditions could be ignored with serious results; in the second part we see how an official who had made a careful study of the native beliefs and traditions, could prevent mischief.

> Ashanti remained very unsettled after the deportation of the King [Prempeh] but might well have been pacified but for one fatal blunder. The most treasured possession of the Ashanti Nation is the Golden Stool. To Ashantis it is more than a symbol of the unity of the people under the authority of the King. It is regarded as the repository of the soul of the

nation and its preservation is a solemn duty to their ancestors, as much as to their posterity.

In 1899 Sir Frederic Hodgson conceived the idea of attempting to gain possession of the Stool and an unsuccessful search was made for it in the following year. The Governor then visited Kumasi personally and demanded the surrender of the Stool. A further search was started. In less than a week the Ashantis rose in arms and the Governor and his garrison were besieged in Kumasi. The Governor and his party escaped and the garrison which remained, after anxious months, was finally relieved and the Ashantis subdued.

The construction of a road in 1921 resulted in the removal of the Stool from its hiding place to a house in a nearby village. There certain Ashantis, including a guardian of the Stool, stripped it of its gold and ornaments and began to sell them. They were caught. The Chief Commissioner, following the advice of Captain Rattray, a District Commissioner, who had made a study of Ashanti history, assembled the Kumasi Chiefs and informed them that the Government made no claim whatever to the Stool. He handed over the offenders for trial by the Chiefs.

This action eventually resulted in the repaired Golden Stool being brought out of hiding and it features prominently to-day in the official celebrations of the Asantehene, the Chief to whom Ashanti owes allegiance and the successor of Prempeh who was exiled in 1896.

It is not surprising that during the nineteenth century with the fluctuating policy of the home Government, hardly any advance was made in the Gold Coast in bringing the Africans themselves into the work of administration. The little that was done can be attributed to the beneficent rule of George Maclean when the colony was left to look after itself for fifteen years; his achievement can be paralleled in other parts of the Empire. The Crown Governor was supported by a Legislative Council of British officials until 1916; the first step was then taken towards broadening the administration; three Europeans and six Africans (including three chiefs) were added to the Council by nomination.

The next step was taken in 1925 when the elective principle was introduced; out of the twenty-nine members of the Council, fourteen were elected; of these nine were Africans, three of whom were elected by the municipalities of Accra,

Cape Coast, and Sekondi, and six by the Provincial Councils of Chiefs that had also been established. In 1927 the important principle was laid down that the traditional authority and customs should be observed as far as possible in the administration.

The new constitution in 1946 established a Legislative Council containing a majority of elected native members. This proved a temporary stage of development. Thousands of men who had served in the second World War outside their native land, came home with a desire for a larger share in the government of their country. Their ideas greatly influenced public opinion. A Committee on Constitutional Reform was appointed to consider what should be the next step towards self-government. This Committee was representative of all sections of the population. Its Report was presented to the Governor in August 1949, and, two months later, the Secretary of State for the Colonies accepted the main proposals on behalf of H.M. Government.

It is not possible here to set out the details of this new constitution; it provides for local government, for regional administration, and for a central legislature. One change in nomenclature is significant; the former 'Native Authorities' are now called 'Local Authorities.' The local franchise is given to adults who have paid their local tax and have been in residence for six months. The first elections were held in 1950.

On the administration of the law, the 1947 Report says:

> The Native Courts are of four grades ranging from the petty village court to the highest grade court which may well serve a population of 100,000 persons.... The law administered is the customary African law so long as it is not incompatible with natural justice, equity and good conscience and, in so far as criminal cases are concerned, so long as it is an offence prescribed as cognisable by Native Courts.

There are 348 Native Courts in the three territories; during 1946–7 they dealt with 68,730 cases.

It is impossible here to give an adequate conception of the

work done in the colony for education, public health, housing and social welfare. The task is of great proportions but much has already been achieved and the plans for future development are ambitious. The advances made in industry, trade and public services are equally considerable.

The pioneer work in education was done by the missions, and they continue this excellent form of service; the Government has done much already to increase the number of schools and, of equal importance, the opportunities for being trained as teachers. The vernacular is the medium of instruction with English as a main subject.

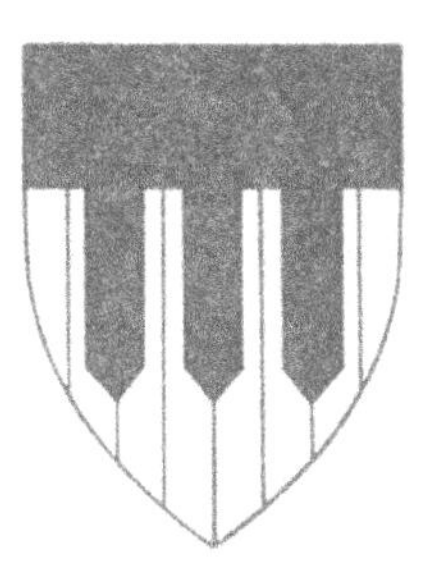

Badge of Achimota College near Accra, Gold Coast.

One college in the Gold Coast has an international fame; the Prince of Wales School and College, Achimota (near Accra), owes much to the work of a great African, Dr Aggrey, who died in 1927. His devotion to the education of his people captured the enthusiasm of many outside his own country, and Achimota College may well be regarded as his monument. He was a warm advocate of close co-operation between the British and the Africans; he used to illustrate the need for this by taking the piano as a text. "You can", he said, "play a tune of sorts on the white keys, and you can play a tune of sorts on the black keys, but for harmony you must use both the black and the white." This saying of his suggested the design for the badge of Achimota College.

## iii. *Responsibility*

We are not responsible for the government of the Dominions but we have to play our part in maintaining good relations and developing the spirit of the Commonwealth. We are more directly responsible for the government of the colonies.

The table on p. 197 shows how this chain of responsibility is linked up.

A greater sense of concern by the Government was shown by the Colonial Development and Welfare Act of 1940 which made substantial grants towards the colonies; these were increased in 1945. Their purpose is to make possible further developments in social services and welfare as well as in industry. Private capital is no longer available for such purposes, and, indeed, could not meet the growing need, for much of the work to be done is unproductive in the commercial sense.

The colonies arrange their own finances; they make no contribution to the United Kingdom apart from any mutual trading benefits; they are free to trade with any country and to make the most advantageous agreements they can.

Reference has already been made to the advice provided through the Colonial Office; training for the colonial service is now directed along sound lines; great emphasis is put, for instance, on a knowledge of native customs and traditions as well as on languages.

A further means of pooling knowledge and experience regionally is provided by the Central African Council (the Rhodesias and Nyasaland) set up in 1944, and the East and West African Governors' Conferences.

Trusteeship Territories (of which Tanganyika is the most important) are subject to the supervision of the Trusteeship Council of the United Nations; annual reports are submitted to this and complaints are examined; missions are sent out to study local administration and to suggest future developments.

Our responsibility should not cease when we have elected our member of Parliament; colonial affairs rarely become prominent during general elections. The case of Palestine (which was a Mandated or Trusteeship Territory) was exceptional in rousing much public concern. Our members of Parliament realise that they have responsibilities towards the

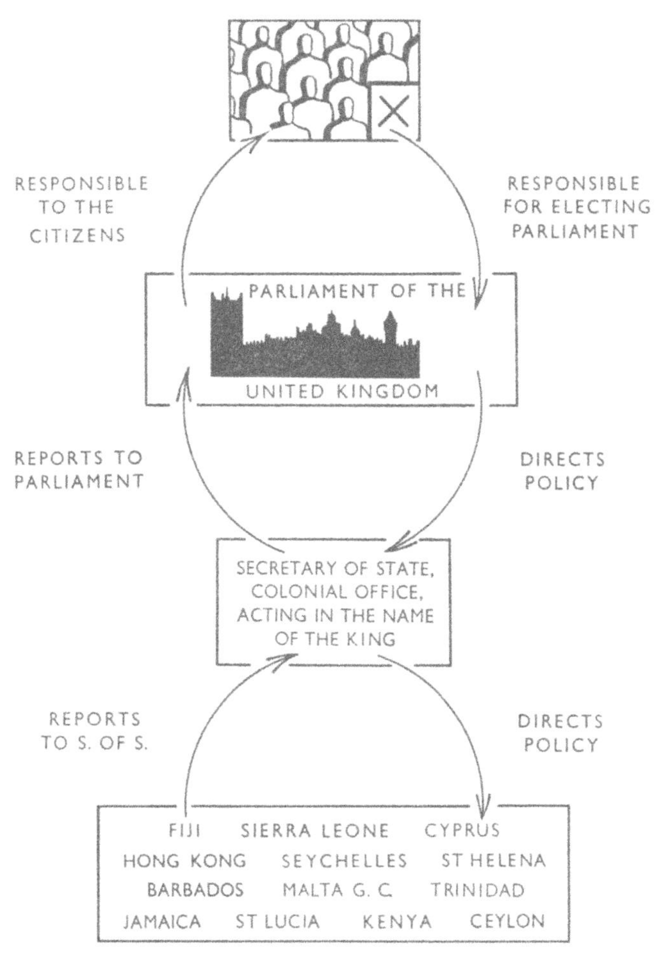


*The bottom rectangle contains the names of representative colonies, etc.*

Colonies, and do not hesitate to ask questions of the Secretary of State. How alive they are to this may be shown by the subjects on which questions were asked on one day; the following were amongst the topics raised: electricity schemes in Nigeria, soil erosion in Africa, European settlement in Tanganyika, social services in Trinidad, industrial development of the West Indies, police force in Malaya, education in Sierra Leone, and corporal punishment in Nigerian prisons.

Some people talk with regret of the 'dissolution' of the British Empire; as our aim for many decades has been the training of peoples towards self-government, this so-called dissolution is inevitable, otherwise our whole policy is frustrated. The process is not finished but in the course of it we are evolving a new kind of association of peoples intent on peace amongst themselves and on developing a higher standard of culture and of living; the closeness of the bond between them and us will vary from country to country, but that bond remains strong and may well become stronger.

This new conception has been well expressed by Compton Mackenzie in a diary (*All over the Place*) of a post-war tour to the East. During a visit to Burma, he noted:

> On a sidewalk near the quay at Moulmein there is a statue of Queen Victoria sitting under a stone canopy illuminated by a solitary electric lamp. This was erected in 1897 to commemorate the Diamond Jubilee. The Queen has her back to the quay and now surveys, sceptre and orb in hand, the ruins of bombed Government offices on the other side of the road...In exactly fifty years the decline and fall of the British Empire has been consummated. Queen Victoria in Moulmein eyes the ruins. The great Commonwealth we optimists hope to see emerge from the ashes, if peace be granted to the world for another fifty years, will have little in common with the British Empire. Nevertheless, the foundation of that Commonwealth will be that old British Empire, and I found in that solitary lamp alight over the head of Queen Victoria an omen of its vitality in the future.

CHAPTER XXII

# HOW WE CAN HELP

The first problem is to get at the facts so that we know what we are talking about. Information about constitutions with statistics is given in *Whitaker's Almanack* (the complete edition only), and in *The Statesman's Year Book*. A study group should possess a copy of the first; the second should be in every public library.

A good general survey, with useful maps, is given in *Origins and Purpose: a Handbook of the British Commonwealth and Empire* (H.M.S.O.). Greater detail is found in *The British Empire* (Oxford University Press) produced under the authority of the Royal Institute of International Affairs. The information in this and similar books may be out-of-date in some details.

H.M.S.O. publishes annual reports on the colonies; there are about fifty of these; each contains the latest information with a brief history, maps and pictures. There is unfortunately no atlas of the Commonwealth and Empire, but the available historical atlases are helpful in tracing developments of territory. Groups will find the large maps published by H.M.S.O. most useful. Knowing where a colony or Dominion is situated, its general configuration, etc., is the first piece of knowledge to acquire.

Most books on this subject refer to such documents as the Durham Report on Canada and the Statute of Westminster. The serious reader is advised to study these in the original wording and not be content with summaries. Two sets have been conveniently published in the World's Classics; both were edited by Professor Berriedale Keith; *Selected Speeches and Documents in British Colonial Policy, 1763–1917*, is in two volumes; *Speeches and Documents on the British Dominions, 1918–1931*, is a single volume.

Three short books in the 'Current Problems' Series, published by the Cambridge University Press, will be found stimulating: *The Ideas and Ideals of the British Empire* by Sir Ernest Barker; *Colonies* by E. A. Walker; *An Exposition of Empire* by C. E. Carrington.

Lord Lugard's *The Dual Mandate in British Tropical Africa* (Blackwood), and Lord Hailey's *African Survey* (Oxford University Press) have a wider application than their titles suggest.

For those who are attracted by the historical side of the subject a good beginning is provided by Basil Williams's *The British Empire 1585–1942* (Home University Library). This might be followed by J. A. Williamson's *Short History of British Expansion* (Macmillan, two vols). The first volume deals with the old Colonial Empire, and the second with modern times.

It is difficult to select books on particular Dominions and colonies as there are so many that are worth reading. A few are mentioned in *Origins and Purpose* (see above); any librarian will gladly give advice on others.

The individual reader may find the following suggestions helpful:

1. What do we mean by 'Empire' and 'Commonwealth'? Do you think 'British Commonwealth and Empire' the best term?
2. Compare the constitution of Canada with that of South Africa. Why is the first federal and the second unitary?
3. In what ways has each World War hastened developments in Commonwealth and Empire relations?
4. What arguments would you use to convince a foreigner that the Dominions are really sovereign states?
5. Do you think a Federal Parliament (or Commonwealth Parliament) at Westminster is desirable, and if so, practicable? Suggest a constitution for it.
6. Study and compare the careers and achievements of Sir Stamford Raffles and Cecil Rhodes.
7. Some people prefer the word 'partnership' to 'trusteeship' in speaking of the Empire. What is your opinion?

8. "We may truly maintain that in its origin and essence our Empire has been neither aggressive nor tyrannous: that it has sprung from honourable beginnings, and that it has made for the happiness and progress of the people whom it includes" (W. H. Hadow, *Citizenship*, p. 149). Consider the justice of this statement.

9. Study the history of Newfoundland as an example of the changing fortunes of a one-time Dominion.

10. How, if at all, should we use such words as: nigger, negro, native, black, white, coloured, half-caste?

## For group or team study the following suggestions may be considered.

1. Each member to make a study of one Dominion. A series of talks, comparisons and discussions should follow dealing with such subjects as constitutions, immigration policies, trade relations, labour problems, defence, etc.

2. Each member to study one colony (using the Annual Report as a basis) or a group of contiguous colonies such as the West Indies. Group talks and discussions would deal with indirect rule, the dual mandate, work of missions, social services, etc.

3. "The British Empire is the surest bulwark against war in the present-day world" (A. Zimmern, *The Third British Empire*, p. 66). That statement was written in 1934; five years later war broke out. Discuss this.

4. Hold a mimic Imperial Conference on current Commonwealth problems.

5. Discuss the Statute of Westminster.

6. Get a copy of the British Nationality Act, 1948 (H.M.S.O., *6d.*). Discuss its application to various parts of the British community.

7. Hold a mimic meeting of the Trusteeship Council; one member should make a complaint and another speak for the United Kingdom. At a meeting of the Council in June 1948, a Uganda spokesman said that there "is no single African territory in which the British train people for self-government". This might be the topic of the meeting.

8. Discuss "The Dominion in which I should choose to settle".

9. Get a copy of the Careers pamphlet on the Colonial Service (H.M.S.O., *4d.*). Discuss the kind of training best suited for such work.

10. Collect from Hansard for one month (each member taking a week) questions asked in the House of Commons on colonial affairs. Study the answers. Draw up a list of five questions the group would like to ask the Secretary of State.

# THE WORLD COMMUNITY

## CHAPTER XXIII

## THE LEAGUE OF NATIONS

The desire for the peaceful settlement of differences between States is by no means modern. In 1625 a Dutchman, Grotius, published a book *On the Laws of Peace and War*. He felt compelled to deal with the subject as he looked around him and saw the devastation caused throughout Europe by the religious wars of the seventeenth century. The English Quaker, William Penn, in 1693, published his *Essay on European Peace*. In this he proposed the formation of a Parliament of States for the settlement of disputes. The suggestion was ignored at the time, but it now reads with a curiously modern tone. During the eighteenth century a number of other projects were put forward, the most important of which were those of the Abbé de St Pierre's *Project for Perpetual Peace* (1712), Rousseau's *A Lasting Peace* (1761), Jeremy Bentham's *International Tribunal* (1786), and Kant's *Towards Perpetual Peace* (1795). Although nothing concrete resulted from these schemes they all served to point the way towards some kind of agreement amongst States, and so prepared the ground for future work.

In the world of politics during the nineteenth century there was, however, some progress towards an international organisation. In 1815 the Russian Czar, Alexander I, put forward a scheme for a Holy Alliance by which he hoped that the Governments of Europe would unite in the principles of Christianity and that the heads of the States would meet together regularly for discussion of common interests. Much ridicule has been poured upon this scheme, but it must be understood that as originally proposed by Alexander it was never seriously considered and that its place was taken by an alliance between Russia, Prussia, Austria, England and France. Another Russian Czar, Nicholas II, was responsible for the most important step taken during the nineteenth century towards a European International Court. He proposed a Peace Conference in 1898, and it first met at the Hague in the following year, with the result that a permanent Court of Arbitration was set up, and during the following years much valuable work was done in settling differences between nations. The weakness of this Court lay in the fact that only relatively unimportant disputes were referred to it and it could only give opinions on matters of fact. It was in no sense a Court of Justice. Its members were drawn from a list of names submitted by the various Governments who had signed the Convention. Where arbitration was acceptable the disputants selected from that list of names the arbitrators by whose decisions they were willing to abide.

Arbitration, however, was becoming a recognised way of dealing with international disputes. One of the best examples is that of the *Alabama* case of 1862–72. This related to the ship *Alabama* which was allowed by the British Government to leave a British port and to take part in the American Civil War on the side of the South. When the war was over the United States made a claim against this country for the damage caused by the *Alabama*, and in consequence the relations between the two countries became very strained. The matter, however, was submitted for arbitration to a tribunal at Geneva and Britain accepted the decision, and paid over £3,000,000 for damages. Commenting on this case, Gladstone said, "I regard the fine imposed on this country as dust in the balance compared with the moral value of the example set when these two great nations...went in peace and concord before a judicial tribunal rather than resort to the arbitrament of the sword".

## i. *Forming the League*

But although isolated cases such as that just described stand out by reason of their rarity, there was no machinery in existence for dealing adequately with the situation which suddenly arose in Europe in August 1914. When the horrors of that war had been realised men felt that if only there had been some means of delaying mobilisation, the matters in dispute could have been settled without bloodshed, and during the war itself a number of eminent statesmen began to consider the possibility of establishing a League of Nations. Soon after the outbreak of war, a group of public men discussed the problem of international peace, and in March 1915 a League of Nations Society was established. In 1916, Lord Robert Cecil, Under-Secretary at the Foreign Office, drafted the first official paper on the subject; this was the basis of all later discussions and plans. Similar work was going on in the United States of America. In June 1918 Lloyd George declared, "We must seek by the creation of some international organisation to limit the burden of armaments and diminish the probability of war". Woodrow Wilson, the President of the United States, included the formation of "a general association of nations" in the Fourteen Points which were the basis of the peace terms. This ensured its discussion and led ultimately to the creation of the League.

The Peace Conference of 1919 appointed a Commission to consider the possibility of drawing up a scheme for a League of Nations. The constitution and functions of the League as suggested by that Commission were adopted by the Peace Conference and incorporated in the treaties of peace. The League formally came into existence on 10 January 1920. It held its last meeting on 18 April 1946, and the United Nations took its place.

We too readily say "The League failed" and so dismiss from our consideration one of the most remarkable experiments made by mankind. It is true that the League did not prevent a major war; yet that is not the right way of putting the matter—whether we speak of 'The League' or 'U.N.O.' we must remember that neither was, nor can be, stronger than the collective will of its members. A single nation, intent on war, ready to risk all in the hope of snatching initial advantage, can wreck any peace machinery.

We should not forget the important humanitarian and economic work achieved by the League; this has continued almost without a break under the authority of the United Nations Organisation. The League developed a new technique in international co-operation and its Secretariat laid the foundations of an international Civil Service. A quarter of a century is a brief period in history; though the League members were not able to preserve peace, they did accomplish a great deal while working together under the impulse of a great ideal.

One of the organisations set up under the League Covenant, the International Labour Organisation, has survived the second World War—perhaps because the limelight was seldom focused on it! This body of representatives of employers and workers sets up standards of labour; these have no legal authority unless a member-State decides to pass the necessary legislation. The Conventions and Recommendations made have undoubtedly influenced social progress in many countries where hitherto capital and labour had been left to fight it out between themselves.

## ii. *The Failure*

It would not be to our purpose here to describe the machinery of the League, nor can we attempt even a summary of its achievements. It will be more helpful to consider the question "Why did the League fail to prevent a second World War?"

A not uncommon answer is to say, "Because the United States of America was not a member". This, it is argued, hamstrung the League from the beginning. The absence of the U.S.A. was certainly a serious handicap, and the refusal of that nation to support the efforts of its own President came as an initial shock from which the League hardly recovered.

Another explanation offered is that the League had no international forces (usually disguised under the less aggressive term 'police') at its command, consequently its bark was worse than its bite. Apart from the considerable practical difficulties of organising such military power, the advocates forget that international law has not the binding force of the statute law of a nation. The nations of the world are in what may be called the Vigilantes stage of law and order (see p. 148); the process of evolving an effective international law (one that can be enforced) must be a long one.

The League provided all the machinery and all the encouragement necessary to prevent war *if its members wished to avoid war.* The failure was not due to defective organisation but to the fact that some of its members deliberately chose war in place of negotiation. If any nation feels strong enough and is inspired with an aggressive patriotism no League can stop war. A war to prevent war is still war.

The development in Italy and Germany of ideals incompatible with the ideals of the League Covenant made war probable. Other nations found it almost impossible to believe, even up to the eleventh hour, that any civilised nation, after the experiences of 1914–18, would wage an aggressive war. The aggressor, like the burglar, always has the initial advantage.

Hopes had also been placed in achieving some measure of agreed disarmament. Commissions and conferences on this thorny subject went on from 1920 to 1935, but no agreement could be reached. No nation was prepared to reduce its forces to any appreciable degree; every possible form of reduction was argued *ad nauseam*—by numbers of men, by categories of weapons, by an all-round percentage, and so on. Actually it was an attempt to put the cart before the horse; no nation will reduce its armed strength unless it feels secure against attack; this sense of insecurity, in spite of the Covenant and Treaties and Pacts, dominated the situation.

The failure of the attempt to stop war in 1935 by the use of economic sanctions against Italy when that country attacked Abyssinia discouraged many supporters of the League. This failure was due to the fact that not all countries joined the scheme (the U.S.A. was not, it must be recalled, a member of the League); some would not apply full sanctions because they feared reprisals—this was not surprising in countries near Italy; others had more sordid reasons for refusing to co-operate. Many had hoped that this economic weapon would prove a substitute for armed force; full participation by all League members might have been effective—we shall never know; but one thing is certain; the imposition of sanctions roused the nationalistic spirit in Italy to a degree beyond the hopes of her rulers. Perhaps had no sanctions been imposed, Italy might have kept out of the second World War—again, we shall never know.

So we come to the rather disheartening conclusion that the League was successful as long as its members were willing to use its machinery, but proved helpless when some decided to go their own way and defy the League.

We have learned much, it may be hoped, from the experience of the League, but there is one lesson that must be repeated again and again. Too many people talked as if the League had been a super-national power above the existing political States that could *make* its members keep the peace. The influence of the League was entirely dependent on the support it had from its members; they, in turn, were dependent on the support each received from public opinion; some found ways of shaping that opinion to a mould devised by a few unscrupulous men. Vigilance is therefore necessary to ensure that public opinion can be freely expressed in all countries; of one thing we can be sure—ordinary folk, and they form the majority, do not want war.

It took several centuries, as we have seen, to establish the King's Peace in this country; such a conception did not arise until late in the twelfth century and it took many years to overcome local prejudices before that Peace was established. In the same way the idea of the Peoples' Peace is strange to many of us, but its establishment must come if war is to end. The League was the first great experiment; we are now engaged in the second experiment—the United Nations Organisation.

CHAPTER XXIV

# THE UNITED NATIONS

This chapter will describe the structure of the United Nations Organisation. Any discussion of its working would be premature, but the reader should familiarise himself with the constitution and functions of each part of the organisation so that he can follow United Nations affairs intelligently.

It should be remembered that the organisation is not something entirely new arising out of the 1939–45 war; it is built on the experience of the League of Nations. The Charter does not mention how much it owes to the Covenant of the League; it is as if all nations were ashamed of a disreputable relative! This is a pity because the success or failure of the United Nations will depend on exactly the same principles as did the League; changed names and improved filing-systems, even new buildings of the most advanced style, will not alter the plain fact that success will depend on the sincerity with which nations seek peace, their probity in observing obligations and their willingness to negotiate one with another: in short, on the acceptance of the principle of 'give and take' that has proved so expedient in this country.

On 25 April 1945 the delegates of fifty nations, representing over 80 per cent of the world's population, met in San Francisco to draw up a Charter for a permanent organisation for the maintenance of peace. They reached agreement on 26 June 1945, and after a sufficient majority of Congresses and Parliaments had ratified the Charter, the United Nations Organisation came into official existence on 24 October 1945. The 24th of October is to be celebrated in future as 'United Nations Day'.

The Charter defines the aims of the United Nations as follows:

To save succeeding generations from the scourge of war;
To reaffirm faith in fundamental human rights;
To establish justice and respect for international obligations, and
To promote social progress and better standards of life.[1]

The following seven principles are then set down:

I. The United Nations is based on the sovereign equality of all its members.

II. Each member shall fulfil its obligations under the Charter, in good faith.

III. All members shall settle disputes by peaceful means and in such a manner that peace, security and justice are not endangered.

IV. No member shall use force or threat of force against the territory or the independence of any state or in any manner not consistent with the purposes of the United Nations.

V. No member should help any state against which the United Nations is taking enforcement action, and all shall support the organisation in any action that it takes in accordance with the Charter.

VI. The United Nations shall ensure that states which are not members act in accordance with these principles as far as is necessary for the maintenance of peace and security.

VII. The United Nations will not intervene in matters which are essentially within the domestic jurisdiction of any state, or compel any member to submit such matters to settlement by the United Nations: a principle which will not apply when coercive measures are applied in order to deal with threats to the peace, breaches of the peace and acts of aggression.[1]

Now if all those principles were genuinely accepted there would be no need for an organisation to guard their practice,

[1] These are not quotations from the Charter but paraphrases.

but in case any nation is tempted to cause trouble the United Nations has established six principal organs with power to set up subsidiary organs.

1. *The General Assembly.* All members of the United Nations are represented on the Assembly. There is one annual session and others if necessary. The President is elected from amongst the members at each session. Decision on important matters is by a two-thirds majority; less important questions are settled by majority vote.

2. *The Security Council.* This is the driving force of the United Nations. Of its eleven members, five are permanent, namely, China, France, the United Kingdom, the Union of Soviet Socialist Republics, and the United States of America. The six non-permanent members are elected for periods of two years by the General Assembly. The Council is in permanent session. The position of President is taken in turn for a month at a time. The voting on the Council raises a difficult question. In the League all decisions (apart from matters of precedure) had to be unanimous to be effective. In the Security Council minor matters, e.g. precedure, can be decided if seven members agree. For more important questions, that is for all things that really matter, there must be an affirmative majority of seven, but (and this is the important point) this seven must include all the five permanent members; so if one of them says 'No', nothing can happen. This is the Veto on which opinion is so divided. Where one of the five permanent members is a party to a dispute, that member may not vote.

3. *The Economic and Social Council.* This consists of eighteen members elected by the General Assembly. It meets at least three times a year; decisions are by simple majority. The President is elected by this Council for a period of one year. The scope of its work is wide; it gives its attention to the following matters amongst others: higher standards of living, economic and social progress, cultural and educational co-operation, the fundamental freedoms. It was under the aegis

of this Council that the Declaration of Human Rights quoted in Chapter 1 was framed.

4. *Trusteeship Council.* This consists of the five permanent members with representatives of other members who administer trust territories and in addition an equal number of members who do not administer such territories. It meets at least twice a year and elects its own President for each session. Decisions are by simple majority. Reference has already been made to the work of this Council (see p. 186).

5. *International Court of Justice.* This is a development of the Permanent Court of International Justice established by the League Covenant. Fifteen judges are elected by the combined wisdom of the Assembly and the Security Council from lists of proposed members; they must be jurists of the highest standing. The President is elected by the Court for a period of three years. Nine judges are sufficient to constitute the Court. Decisions are by simple majority. It sits at the Peace Palace at The Hague and is in permanent session.

6. *The Secretariat.* It is hardly necessary to say anything about this organ; the Secretary-General is appointed by the Assembly on the recommendation of the Security Council. He is given a free hand (within financial limits) in organising the work. The first Secretary-General was Mr Trygve Lie (Norway).

There is, of course, as in all international organisations, a whole galaxy of committees, sub-committees, and so on; some are permanent and others are formed for special purposes. Note should be made of three allied organisations.

*The United Nations Relief and Rehabilitation Administration (U.N.R.R.A.)* did valuable work from the end of the war until the middle of 1947 in dealing with the Displaced Persons and other unfortunates who had been taken to Germany and other countries for enforced labour. This organisation was later succeeded by the International Relief Organisation.

*The Food and Agriculture Organisation* (*F.A.O.*) has had to face the situation created by depleted food supplies and a constantly increasing need. Its first Director-General was Sir John Boyd Orr. It has no legislative powers but it makes known the need and suggests how this can be met.

*The United Nations Educational, Scientific and Cultural Organisation* (*U.N.E.S.C.O.*) was created to promote cultural relations between countries—education, the theatre, music, films, broadcasting, exchange of scientific information, and so on. The first Director-General was Dr Julian Huxley.

The Charter of the United Nations permits the making of regional agreements between countries for the furtherance of peace. In May 1949, the Council of Europe was set up by Denmark, France, the Irish Republic, Italy, Luxembourg, the Netherlands, Norway, Sweden and the United Kingdom. Other European countries are invited to join. The Council consists of a Committee of Ministers (i.e. for Foreign Affairs), and a Consultative Assembly which submits recommendations to the Committee. The members of the Assembly are not spokesmen for their Governments; thus the United Kingdom sent representatives of its three main political parties to the first session held at Strasbourg in August 1949. The Council has no legislative powers, but no Government can afford to ignore its recommendations. The subjects discussed at the first session included: housing, emigration, refugees, patents, and the possibility of a European passport. Matters of National Defence are outside the scope of the Council.

One of the values of the Council of Europe is that it is more local than the United Nations, and we can feel a more direct concern in its discussions.

Finally, it must be emphasised again that the success of the United Nations and of the Council of Europe depends ultimately on the intelligent support of all citizens of the member States. Our Country, our National Community, is a member of both organisations; that means—OURSELVES.

CHAPTER XXV

# HOW WE CAN HELP

The individual citizen feels more helpless in international affairs than in any other of his public concerns. He hears of conference after conference yielding little solid result; all the time he is haunted by a sense of insecurity. What can he do?

It sounds rather dull and unenterprising to repeat the advice that keeping oneself informed is of primary importance. The newspaper should be read—not always the same one—but not too much alarm should be felt at the word 'crisis': this is jargon for anything out of the normal course of events. Comments in the weekly journals are useful guides to different interpretations put on events—again assuming that we do not restrict ourselves to the same journal week by week; a comparison of the views expressed by two or more in the same week is a useful exercise. Broadcast news is, fortunately, confined to facts, except when 'Our Diplomatic Correspondent' has his views quoted. The talks by experts on international affairs should be listened to with attention.

It would be possible to give a long list of helpful books, but a few will suffice to set the reader on his way.

G. M. Gathorne-Hardy's *Short History of International Affairs* (Oxford University Press) covers the period 1920 to 1939. This should be supplemented by a study of original documents given in *Speeches and Documents on International Affairs, 1918–1937*, edited by Professor Berriedale Keith (World's Classics, two vols). The first volume contains the Treaty of Versailles and the League Covenant.

### THE LEAGUE OF NATIONS

A stimulating discussion of the League is given in Sir Alfred Zimmern's *The League of Nations and the Rule of Law*

(Macmillan). Lord Cecil's *A Great Experiment* (Jonathan Cape) is a valuable account by one who played a large part in League affairs.

THE UNITED NATIONS

*The United Nations* by Louis Dolivet (Phoenix) is a clear account of the principles and machinery of the Organisation. H.M.S.O. publishes various booklets (some prepared by the United Nations staff) which help to explain how the Organisation works.

In order to keep in touch with developments and problems, the reader should seek the assistance of The United Nations Association (11 Maiden Lane, London, W.C. 2). *Whitaker's Almanack* summarises each year's meetings.

Here are some suggestions and problems for both individual readers and for groups.

1. Do you think that had the U.S.A. been a member of the League, the second World War would have been impossible?

2. Why should five Powers be permanent members of the Security Council? Should not all nations be on an equal footing?

3. What is the objection to a simple majority decision in all matters? Discuss the working of the Veto.

4. How can the opinions of ordinary people find expression in the United Nations Organisation?

5. Make a comparison between the Covenant of the League and the Charter of the United Nations and discuss the differences.

6. Is such a regional pact as the North Atlantic Treaty in keeping with United Nations principles?

7. Do you think some kind of Federal Union of nations would be (*a*) desirable, and if so, (*b*) practicable?

8. In August 1945 the first atomic bomb was dropped on Hiroshima; two months before that date the Charter of the United Nations had been drawn up. Discuss the effect of the bomb on the Charter!

9. In August 1947 the World Federation of United Nations Associations passed this resolution:

> "That a general agreement should be adopted immediately outlawing the use by all nations of atomic and bacteriological arms and similar means of mass destruction; and that at the same time there should be

> established a system of international inspection and supervision sufficiently comprehensive to make possible the destruction of existing arms or their surrender to an international body."

Discuss the problems raised by the above resolution.

10. Lord Cecil of Chelwood has written:

> "The principle of war, which is an appeal to brute force, to the animal instincts of man, is inconsistent with his spiritual nature. It can only be abolished by acceptance of Christian doctrine and Christian morality" (*All the Way*, 1949, p. 252).

Discuss the above statement.

11. The Council of Europe has no legislative powers, nor are its decisions binding on the member States. What then is its value? Is it just another talking-shop?

12. What subjects would you propose for discussion at the next meeting of the Assembly of the Council of Europe?

# INDEX

*Dates following names of Sovereigns give the years of reigns.*

# INDEX

## INDEX

INDEX

INDEX

INDEX

INDEX

For EU product safety concerns, contact us at Calle de José Abascal, 56–1°,
28003 Madrid, Spain or eugpsr@cambridge.org.

www.ingramcontent.com/pod-product-compliance
Ingram Content Group UK Ltd.
Pitfield, Milton Keynes, MK11 3LW, UK
UKHW042209180425
457623UK00011B/110

* 9 7 8 1 1 0 7 6 1 7 9 0 2 *